Letters from the Boys

Letters from the Boys

Wisconsin World War I Soldiers
Write Home

Carrie A. Meyer

WISCONSIN HISTORICAL SOCIETY PRESS

Published by the Wisconsin Historical Society Press
Publishers since 1855

The Wisconsin Historical Society helps people connect to the past by collecting, preserving, and sharing stories. Founded in 1846, the Society is one of the nation's finest historical institutions.
Join the Wisconsin Historical Society: wisconsinhistory.org/membership

Photographs identified with WHi or WHS are from the Society's collections; address requests to reproduce these photos to the Visual Materials Archivist at the Wisconsin Historical Society, 816 State Street, Madison, WI 53706.

Front cover image: WHi Image ID 88625; back cover image: WHi Image ID 87505
Printed in the United States of America
Designed by Shawn Biner

22 21 20 19 18   1 2 3 4 5

Library of Congress Cataloging-in-Publication Data applied for.

♾ The paper used in this publication meets the minimum requirements of the American National Standard for Information Sciences—Permanence of Paper for Printed Library Materials, ANSI Z39.48-1992.

Contents

Acknowledgments

When I began reading the Green County newspapers with the letters this book is based on, I had little idea where the project would take me. I had something more academic in mind, but the words of these young men pulled me in. In the end I needed to tell their story in their own words. Thus my biggest debt is to them— to the young men, and some women, now all deceased, who wrote the letters.

For the sake of clarity and to smooth the way for the reader, I have made minor edits of the letters I found, and sometimes I have omitted short passages without calling attention to it with ellipses. In general I was astonished at the quality of the letters and I changed very little. But sometimes newspaper editors and typesetters had clearly introduced spelling errors when the handwritten letters were transcribed and printed a hundred years ago. Sometimes I made slight changes in punctuation or wording to increase clarity. Sometimes there were passages that I omitted either because they added little of relevance or contained material that would only confuse readers of this book. In the end, however, the letters reflect the writing style of the original authors—grammatical nuances that did not sacrifice clarity were not corrected—and remain true to the intent of those who wrote them. Racialist terms, that would be found offensive today, were also retained; it is the reader's perogative to judge those who used them.

The Wisconsin Historical Society (WHS) deserves an enormous debt of gratitude for making this project possible and for bringing it to publication. The letters were all published in newspapers that were preserved on microfilm by the society. Even in these digital days, the small-town newspapers on microfilm are a wonderful treasure. The bulk of the photos included here are also from the WHS archives, and many of my sources were housed in the WHS library. Many thanks to the archives and the library staff, and my sincere appreciation to the staff of the Wisconsin Historical Society Press. John Zimm, in particular, has ably guided and shaped the final product with sensitivity and skill, even drafting short passages when I was at a loss for words.

Members and officers of local historical societies in Green County made time to talk to me and help find pictures. I'd like to thank Betty Earlywine of the Brodhead Historical Society, Barbara Pierce and Susan McCallum with the Brooklyn Area Historical Society, Roger Dooley with the Monticello Area Historical Society, and Kim Tschudy, a reporter for the *Monticello Messenger*.

The Provost's Office and the Economics Department at George Mason University deserve thanks for the study leave that allowed me to launch the research for this book in 2011–2012. Kristen Donahue and Jill Scharl provided research assistance in some of the early stages of the project. Lindsey Hillgartner and Russell P. Horton, archivists at the Wisconsin Veterans Museum, also provided generous assistance. Janet Niewold and her family provided hospitality on several occasions while I was in Madison doing research. Jean Schaible read the manuscript in its early stages and encouraged me to get it published.

Finally, the project would not have been completed without the interest and guidance of my husband, Ernie Carlson. Every step of the way he helped by reading letters, discussing where to go with them, encouraging me to get on with it, reading and rereading chapters of the manuscript, and even helping to select appropriate photographs from the WHS and Wisconsin Veterans Museum collections. His insights and moral support were invaluable and added enormous pleasure to the project.

Introduction

World War I was a difficult war for Americans to come to grips with, and this was especially true for the people of Wisconsin. Few supported entry into the war, and enormous sacrifices were required.

Woodrow Wilson had won the presidency in 1916 promising to keep America out of war; the vast majority of Americans wanted little part of it. But in Wisconsin, 30 to 40 percent of the population was German by birth or extraction, and this group had even more reason to oppose it. The strong antiwar position of Wisconsin's popular Senator Robert M. La Follette was well known. When Congress eventually declared war, La Follette was one of only six senators to vote against it. Moreover, in the House of Representatives, nine out of fifty negative votes were from Wisconsin. It's not so surprising that Wisconsin's loyalty was questioned.[1]

Yet when it came time to pitch in, Wisconsin shouldered its share of the burden and more, eagerly proving its patriotism and loyalty. It was the first state to organize a State Council of Defense, the state-level mechanism to muster resources for the war effort. Only 2 percent of the eligible Wisconsin boys failed to register for the draft. In the United States as a whole, the number was more than four times that. Wisconsin readied its National Guard troops early and well. Wisconsin factories worked overtime on war contracts. Wisconsin farmers responded to the demands for more food. Wisconsin women took the place of men in the factories and joined Red Cross circles to make hospital garments and surgical dressings. Wisconsin families observed "meatless" and "wheatless" days to conserve food, six weeks before a similar plan was put into effect for the country as a whole. Wisconsin communities sent their physicians; fully 27 percent of those registered to practice in the state went into military service. And when Wisconsin's citizens bought Liberty Loans to finance the war effort, they exceeded the quotas requested of them.[2]

It is often said the United States arrived late on the scene in World War I and didn't do much fighting. Casualties were light compared to figures for other countries. But that is only because the loss of life and limb was so enormous elsewhere. The United States mobilized 4.4 million troops; approximately 16 percent of the male labor force was inducted into the armed services. Nearly five thousand governmental war agencies were created. At its height, the war absorbed about 23 percent of total economic output in the United States.[3] During their relatively brief time at the western front, the Americans fought hard and helped turn the tide of war against Germany. About 120,000 Americans lost their lives to the war effort, either on the battlefield or from disease, between the end of May and November 1918; an additional 206,000 suffered wounds.[4]

In the final tally, Wisconsin lost more lives per thousand population than the country as a whole. When Wisconsin's Gold Star list was compiled of the soldiers, sailors, marines, and nurses who died in the federal service during the war, 3,972 names appeared. The rate per thousand population was 1.53 compared to 1.16 for the United States overall.[5]

The war was also difficult to come to grips with because new technologies revolutionized the way war was waged and made it much more deadly. Many applications of the internal combustion engine were tested on the battlefield for the first time with considerable success. Trucks and automobiles changed the way that troops, munitions, provisions, and wounded soldiers were transported. Tanks lumbered across the battlefield like great "monsters of the trenches."[6] Submarines and airplanes added new dimensions to the battlefields. Gasoline engines powered new searchlights that lit up the night sky. It was awesome; soldiers and those at home had to marvel at such enormous change.[7] At the same time, however, new technologies increased the horror of war. Trench warfare was the new normal. Men went "over the top" to be mowed down by machine guns. The new high-explosive artillery shells were far more deadly than nineteenth-century cannonballs. Lethal mustard and chlorine gases were also delivered in shells. During the four years of war, at least 16 million men died from all countries and another 20 million were wounded.[8]

For most Americans it was the "letters from the boys" that contributed most to their understanding of what was going on "over there." Yes, the Councils of Defense had patriotic propaganda machines going full blast. And yes, the letters were censored. But the words in the letters were those of boys they were connected to. People who did not have sons or daughters overseas had other relatives or neighbors who did. And all across the country, hometown newspapers printed "letters from the boys."

The smaller the town, the more intimate were the community relationships; these letters made front-page news in small-town America. Sometimes the boys wrote directly to the editor, but more often than not, relatives passed the letters along so that friends and neighbors could share in the news from beloved sons and daughters of the community.

The fact that they were published makes them available today, and the Wisconsin Historical Society has an extraordinary collection of newspapers preserved on microfilm—even from the smallest of Wisconsin towns going back well before the war began. It is an interesting challenge to make sense of these war letters today.

I came upon World War I letters while doing research for a book on rural history in northern Illinois. I was fascinated to learn that letters written a hundred years ago from the trenches

BRODHEAD, WISCONSIN, WEDNESDAY, NOVEMBER 28, 1917

OUR BOYS AT THE FRONT

Lieutenants G. S. Darby and L. B. Rowe, and Privates Requartte Hahn, Elmer Swann and Wilburt Murphy Write Most Interesting Details of Their Camp Life.

FROM LIEUT. G. S. DARBY

Aero Squadron.
Garden City, L. I., Nov. 18, 1917
Steele & Schempp,
Brodhead, Wis.

Dear Friends:—It has been quite a little while since writing you but in my moving about seem to have lost connection with the Independent Register. I'll forgive you that, however, as some of my own personal mail has had some difficulty in getting to me. I do not know as yet when we will leave here, nor where we may go. One squadron left here recently, we supposed for over seas, but found later they were back in one of the central states.

Have been satisfied in a way with our stay here. Every move is planned for the benefit of the squadrons and every thing seems to indicate advancement, and to rend service sometime.

My stay here was made particularly pleasant by a visit from Mrs. Darby and George. We had a fine time seeing New York, but time and space forbits any details.

Our camp here is about twenty miles from the Pennsylvania Station in New York, and located on the exact spot where Gen. Washington's army was once defeated by the British in the Revolutionary war. The present site of Brooklyn is where on the following day he turned the tables. Our quarters are in good substantial barracks and while we have not the conveniences of a modern home we are very comfortable. Also have plenty to eat. Often we get a little of the extra good things from home as jelly, and never was there a time when those things tasted better.

A few days ago, I accidentally learned that some South Dakota National Guardmen were in Camp Mills, just west of our camp. Inquiries and a short trip brought me to the 147th Machine Gun Company in command of First Lieutenant Lester Kirkpatrick. Seems good to meet some one from home. There probably are more there I might know but hard to find. This is a very large camp and many states are represented.

Have pleasure of knowing Dr. Dodge of Clinton Junction. He will follow us over soon, I think. Just arrived here after a seasoning process at Ft. Riley.

Although to-day is Sunday, you would know it only by a little less activity. On our part, however, that is not the case, as we have had a great deal to do. Don't know when you may hear from me again, but hope to be able to get you a little letter once in a while.

Lieut. G. S. Darby.

FROM WILBERT MURPHY.

Camp MacArthur,
Nov. 17, 1917.

Dear Mr. Schempp:—

Your paper of the 14th has just arrived and before I forget, I must try to write a short letter. Time is a scarce article around here until it dries off.

It is just about time for the "retreat" formation, so I'll have to put away this stuff and get my rifle out for inspection.

Respectfully,
Private Wilbert Murphy.
Co. M, 128th U. S. Inf. N. G.
Camp MacArthur,
Waco, Texas.

FROM REQUARTTE HAHN.

A friend has generously permitted us to make the following extracts from this letter from First Class Private Requartte Hahn:

Supply Co. 121st, Field Artillery.
Camp MacArthur, Waco, Texas.
November 15, 1917.

Dear Friend:

I wish that I could tell you just what an army camp like this one is like; but I am such a poor hand at giving a description that I am afraid you will get a poor idea.

Camp MacArthur covers about twenty-five square miles, and the rifle range attached to it is about twelve square miles, quite an area of land don't you think? With the exception of the land along the river, it is all practically level land. The land along the river is hilly and rocky and the best way for me to explain it to you is to imagine a western movie scene. There is one particular road leading down to the river that I am almost sure I have seen in western movie scenes before. There are some mighty pretty places down here, of course nothing like Wisconsin, but still they are noticeable.

As to the climate, that is one thing I don't like about Texas. Of course it is nice and warm, has not been disagreeably cold since we have been here. But the wind and the dust are something terrible. The dust covers everything and is certainly a fright. My throat has been sore ever since I came here. One just craves for rain, I do anyway for it has not rained since we have been here. I never want to live in Texas. Wisconsin is good enough for me.

And now to give you an idea of the number of men, mules, horses and motor trucks here. There are about 35,000 men in all, and about 7,500 horses and mules. We have 900 animals in our regiment alone, and about 1,000 motor trucks. From seven a. m. to 5:30 p. m. every man animal and truck is doing some form of duty. You can imagine what is going on, hundreds of men drilling on the parade ground. Four-mule teams and motor trucks hauling supplies and one thing I nearly forgot was that one can look up and see army aeroplanes sailing about most any time. Every man, animal and machine is doing its duty in a business like manner and no one is seen loafing around.

The main part of this camp, or the business center is the Quartermaster Department. This is made up of about twenty-five large buildings where all the supplies are received and then issued out to each regiment. It is here where you may see numbers of four-mule teams

fortunately died from sunstroke the other froze to death. This may sound fishy to some of the skeptical, but nevertheless, it represents the true condition of weather here.

Since I was transferred into the Medical Dept. of the 127th Infantry I have enjoyed the most comfortable quarters, and best food any one could reasonably want in the army. We are housed in the regulation pyramidal army tent with following accommodations: Sides boarded up four feet, floor, electric lights, stove and plenty of wood which is brot to us in trucks and sawed by the unfortunates in the guard house. As for food, we eat in dining room of our regimental hospital; are served by two of our men detailed to kitchen duty, and enjoy a well cooked and varied diet. To-day noon (Sunday) we had pork steak, dressing seasoned with sage, baked sweet potatoes, sweet pickles, bread and butter, tea and lemon pie. How could we be anything else but satisfied with such a layout. The success of such a mess lies in good management and co-operation of the cook and mess sergeant.

The last few days something new and interesting occurs daily with clock-like regularity. Friday with several others of our detachment were sent out with a battalion of trench diggers and wire entanglement constructors. We rode out in an ambulance arriving at the trenches at about eight bells. As few men got hurt or sick we wandered about the field where a sham battle is soon to be staged, watching the men build trenches in regular French style; zig zag, with steps sand bags, parapets, and communication lines. Parapets are constructed in front of every piece of trench so that the enemy cannot fire into it from front or flank. I should think that the wire entanglements would be a perfect h—l to climb thru when under heavy rifle fire from covered rifle pits less than a 100 yards back and supported by machine guns. These wires are probably cut in some way or other before an assault, otherwise an attack would be fatal to charging column.

Yesterday (Saturday) our Division (32nd) defeated the Old 2nd Texas; the latter previous to the game being boastingly advertised as the Undefeatable. Score 21 to 0. Walter Tippet, a Lawrence man in our detachment was the star of the game both on defense and offensive. "Moose" Gardner (U. Wis.) broke thru the Texas line on their ten yard line blocking their punt and falling on the ball for a touchdown. Athletics find a prominent part in the development of a soldier. Every Wednesday and Saturday p. m. are given over to games of some sort. Oftentimes numerous games are scheduled on Sunday. By providing the fellows with proper amusement and excitement right in the camp the officers keep the men from the going down town and money-spending craze. At no other time has the welfare of the soldier and his immediate relatives

When the "boys" wrote home to family and friends in Green County, their letters made front-page news. *BRODHEAD INDEPENDENT REGISTER*, NOV 28, 1917

in France addressed "Dear Mother and Father" were so readily available. I was interested in the use of gasoline engines on local farms and the fact that midwestern farmboys took engine skills with them to France in World War I. So I began to explore the letters and incorporate them into my research agenda. But I was even more intrigued by the story that might be told if one could get to know some of these boys a little. That resulted, of course, in this manuscript.

I chose to review all the letters in the newspapers of three small towns in Green County, Wisconsin. Green County is a quintessential Wisconsin rural dairy county, south of Madison and bordering Illinois. A similar manuscript could have been written, perhaps, for any rural community in the Midwest; the choice of Green County was essentially fortuitous. And what I found was fascinating.

The letters began to appear in the fall of 1917 when the Green County newspapers were filled with news of the war and the draft. As young men from the county headed off to military camps, the letters they wrote home made front-page news. Many young men signed up with the National Guard and went to Waco, Texas. Some enlisted with the navy and went to Norfolk, Virginia. Several doctors from Brodhead went to Fort Riley, Kansas. Roger Skinner from the same town was already in France driving a Ford ambulance. A young man from Monticello went off to New Mexico to train with the Minnesota infantry.[9] Others would be drafted weeks or months later. I couldn't follow every story; I had to make choices.

Two stories stood out. While Wisconsin boys went off in all different directions for the war effort, the largest group went with the National Guard to be part of the 32nd Division. The 32nd Division arrived early in France. It distinguished itself on the battlefield, earning the French sobriquet "*Les Terribles.*" The 32nd was also chosen to be part of the army of occupation and followed the German army back into Germany after the armistice. Thus, the first part of this manuscript follows the journey of the Wisconsin National Guard in World War I, as told in letters from a handful of Green County boys. Many of those letters were written by Reuel R. Barlow, a talented young journalist from Monticello.

The second part of the manuscript is composed of the letters of Roger A. Skinner from Brodhead, who volunteered with the ambulance corps and arrived in France in September of 1917, many months before the 32nd. Skinner did not become a well-known writer, as did Ernest Hemingway and Archibald MacLeish, who likewise drove ambulances in World War I. But Skinner was a charming and talented writer. His letters were popular with Green County readers and are still compelling today.

GREEN COUNTY, WISCONSIN, CIRCA 1917

In order to imagine ourselves as readers from Green County, Wisconsin, a little background is necessary.

First of all, remember that most people in the United States lived in rural places at the time of World War I. Not until the 1920 Census did more than half of the US population live in towns with populations greater than 2,500 people. Wisconsin was just slightly more rural than the United States as a whole. Small towns were vibrant places then.[10]

Wisconsin had managed to turn itself into America's leading dairy state in the several decades before the war started. Wisconsin was producing about half of the cheese produced in the United States, and Green County was among the top cheese-producing counties. The county's Swiss colony of New Glarus had produced factory cheese since the time of the Civil War and had developed quite a reputation for the pungent Limburger cheese, popular with the German and Swiss immigrants in the area. By 1911, Green County's cheese industry had grown to produce more than 14 million pounds of cheese annually in 182 factories.[11] Wisconsin was praised by Theodore Roosevelt, among others, as an example of what personal initiative, scientific advancements, and government support working in concert could do.[12]

The farmers in Green County were not country bumpkins; they were the high-tech dairymen of the time. Even before the war, many dairy farmers in the area had built silos and were feeding corn silage to their dairy cattle.[13] Many of them were already driving automobiles, and they used advanced machinery on their farms. Green County farms were fairly large on average—nearly 150 acres—and prosperous.[14] As elsewhere in southern Wisconsin, telephones, electricity, and running water were becoming common on the most prosperous dairy farms.[15]

But Green County was (and still is) a very rural place. Its only town of any size is Monroe, whose population at the time was something under five thousand people. The population of the entire county was under twenty-two thousand.[16]

The letters in this manuscript were printed in the newspapers of just three towns: Brooklyn, Monticello, and Brodhead. Brooklyn and Monticello were officially "villages" in 1913, with populations of approximately 400 and 670, respectively. Brodhead, on the other hand, was classified as a "city" and boasted two newspapers and a population of 1,517.[17] The advertising and other content in the newspapers confirm that all three towns primarily provided services to the surrounding farm families; the papers circulated in the local countryside.

Monticello, in 1917, had many cheese factories as well as a flour mill and a woolen mill. It had two businesses that bought and shipped livestock, two farm equipment dealers, two hardware stores, two blacksmith shops, and two lumber dealers that also offered coal and feed. The town and the surrounding farms also justified three automobile dealerships, a bank, and an attorney's office that sold insurance on the side. Other stores sold

This bird's-eye view of Monticello was captured on a postcard in 1912.
MONTICELLO AREA HISTORICAL SOCIETY

groceries, general merchandise, jewelry and watches, drugs, and hats, and a couple of businesses produced handmade cigars from locally grown tobacco. Finally, the town had an undertaker who also engaged in the furniture business.[18] Brooklyn was similarly known for dairy products and tobacco. The village was composed of general stores, blacksmith shops, a creamery, and a bank as well as a few other businesses. Both towns had four-year high schools, as well as good water systems and electricity.[19]

Brodhead had been a site of considerable productive activity, but it was already past its prime by the time the United States entered World War I. A dam had previously supplied water power for several manufacturing interests: a foundry, several wagon shops, and a plow factory. But all of these had closed. A mill was still used to grind corn meal and feed, and the area took pride in its agriculture—dairy, hogs, and tobacco.[20] The population of

Brodhead was composed largely of retired farmers and retired businessmen, but it was still a vibrant community, with up-to-date stores, a good school system and public library, and a variety of churches and civic societies.[21] Brodhead was the first town in Green County to offer electricity with a generator run by water power from the dam. Brodhead had two newspapers. Its largest, the *Independent Register*, circulated widely in the surrounding rural area; it claimed the largest circulation of any weekly newspaper in southern Wisconsin, reaching more than 2,400 families. The other, the *Brodhead News*, essentially competed for the same audience.

Green County was a homogeneous place at the time of the war: virtually 100 percent white and highly literate. About 15 percent of the population was foreign born; more than half of that was Swiss and another 26 percent German. The foreign-born population was more prevalent on farms. Immigrants made up 25 percent of all farmers in the county.[22]

Before war was declared, Green County was fairly united in its opposition to the war. Monroe, the county seat, had held a referendum on the war as part of the spring election on April 3, 1917. It had the distinction of being the only official referendum on war in the United States. Ninety percent of voters expressed opposition to a declaration of war "under existing circumstances." Three days later when Congress actually declared war, the community staged a mass meeting to pledge loyalty.[23] Similar patriotic rallies were held in cities and towns throughout the state during the month of April 1917. Brodhead also held such a meeting. The editor of the *Independent Register* called it "Brodhead's chance to let the state and country know that we are Americans here." He continued, "Whether we should enter the war or not is no longer an issue. We are at war. The question is, 'Shall I be a slacker, or shall I be fervent in support of my government.' "[24] Wisconsin clearly chose the latter.

PART I

Letters from the Boys of the 32nd

CHAPTER ONE

Stateside

For three years Americans watched from across the Atlantic as Europe was torn apart by the deadliest war the world had yet seen. Though the United States enjoyed strong economic and cultural ties to Allied nations, Americans seemed content to stay out of the war when they reelected President Wilson in 1916 with the slogan "He kept us out of the war." While leaders and the public debated between preparedness and neutrality, until 1917 Wilson chose the latter option.

German submarine attacks ultimately eroded Wilson's resolve to remain neutral. He asked Congress to declare war on Germany on April 6, 1917, and Congress did so four days later. But the country was hardly ready to send men to fight. It had an army of only 220,000 men. By mid-May, newspapers in Green County reported federal plans to raise an army of two million men by volunteers and draft. Eleven million men between the ages of twenty-one and thirty years were subject to the draft. Two drafts of five hundred thousand each were anticipated, and registration began on June 5. Prior to that, volunteers as young as eighteen and as old as forty could enlist with the regular army or the National Guard. Many young men from Green County enlisted with the National Guard.[1]

In order to train the army, the federal government began building thirty-two training camps during the summer of 1917. One of these was Camp MacArthur located near Waco, Texas; it was here that the National Guard troops from Wisconsin and Michigan joined to form the 32nd Division.

CAMP DOUGLAS

While Camp MacArthur was under construction, the Wisconsin National Guard began training at Camp Douglas. The National Guard was called into federal service on Sunday, July 15. On that day about twelve thousand Wisconsin men reported to the armories of their local company to be sent to Camp Douglas, the state military reservation, about ninety miles northwest of Madison.[2] For the Green County boys, this was not so far from home.

Reuel Barlow was among the young men who went to Camp Douglas that Sunday in mid-July. The *Monticello Messenger* reported that he had surprised his friends in Monticello by getting married the previous Thursday to Ruth Leitzell of Freeport, Illinois. Barlow was a journalism student at the University of Wisconsin and already had newspaper experience. He joined the Field Hospital Corps of the Wisconsin National Guard. During the next two years, Barlow would write many letters home to his family that would appear in the *Messenger* and other local papers.[3]

Barlow and the other National Guard troops spent several weeks at Camp Douglas before moving on to Camp MacArthur. The number of men ultimately assembled at Camp Douglas rose to 15,256, including infantry, field artillery, cavalry, engineers, field hospitals, and ambulance companies. Since the federal government was running behind with equipment for the new recruits, the state spent some $780,000 to fully equip the soldiers with uniforms, blankets, and other supplies.[4]

The Wisconsin National Guard troops reported first to Camp Douglas, about ninety miles northwest of Madison. WHI IMAGE ID 132557

A few Wisconsin guardsmen did not make it to Waco. Three companies of men from Fond du Lac, Oshkosh, and Appleton were transferred to the 42nd "Rainbow" Division, so named because it was assembled from National Guard units from twenty-six states. The Rainbow Division trained in New York and arrived in France several weeks before the other Wisconsin guardsmen.[5]

The majority of the Wisconsin National Guard troops, including those from Green County, began traveling by train in September to Waco. The *Brooklyn Teller* ran an article on September 26 that reported on the movement of the Guard troops:

> Five trainloads of troops, on their way from Camp Douglas to Waco, Texas, passed through here on Monday, but made no stops between Madison and Janesville. Eight Brooklyn boys—Ben and Einar Johnson, Thorwald and Bernie Christensen, Otis O'Brien, Frank Milbrandt, Albert Weisser, and Melvin Berger, members of Co. M, 1st regiment—were on the second train; and many relatives and friends went to

Janesville to bid them farewell. Several thousand people took
part in the demonstrations both at Madison and Janesville,
the railroad grounds and nearby streets being thronged with
people anxious for a parting word and hand clasp.[6]

Some of the first letters published "from the boys" were those
written home from the train. Wilbert Murphy wrote to the editor
of the *Brodhead News*, explaining that the troops mailed letters by
throwing them out the car windows as they passed by a station.
"Someone is sure to see them and pick them up and mail them."
He described their breakfast of corned beef hash and potatoes
and the progress of their trip:

> We are in Illinois now, about 190 miles from St Louis and
> 100 miles or more from Chicago. We reached Milwaukee
> last night about 6:30 and were given a grand reception. It
> sounded like all the factory whistles were blowing. Reached
> Chicago at 11:00 p.m. and stayed in the yards until 1:30 this
> morning. Then we must have stopped about fifty times before
> we got out of the "Windy City." Just looking out of the win-
> dow I notice all kinds of corn fields. The land is level and all a
> person can see in places is corn.[7]

CAMP MACARTHUR

Soon letters that described Camp MacArthur and the town of
Waco began appearing in newspapers throughout the state. The
Green County boys who went off to Camp MacArthur wrote
many hundreds of letters home. Dozens of such letters were
printed in the newspapers of Brodhead, Brooklyn, and Monticello. A few of those are presented here.

Requartte Hahn described Camp MacArthur in a letter to a friend, who passed it along to Brodhead's *Independent Register*:

Camp MacArthur covers about twenty-five square miles, and the rifle range attached to it is about twelve square miles. With the exception of the land along the river, it is all practically level land. The land along the river is hilly and rocky and the best way for me to explain it to you is to imagine a western movie scene. There is one particular road leading down to the river that I am almost sure I have seen in western movie scenes before. There are some mighty pretty places down here, of course nothing like Wisconsin, but still they are noticeable.

As to the climate, that is one thing I don't like about Texas. Of course it is nice and warm, has not been disagreeably cold since we have been here. But the wind and the dust are something terrible. The dust covers everything and is certainly a fright. My throat has been sore since I got here. One just craves for rain. I do anyway, for it has not rained since we have been here. I never want to live in Texas. Wisconsin is good enough for me.

And now to give you an idea of the number of men, mules, horses, and motor trucks here. There are about 35,000 men in all, and about 7,500 horses and mules. We have 900 animals in our regiment alone, and about 1,000 motor trucks. From 7:00 a.m. to 5:30 p.m., every man, animal, and truck is doing some form of duty. You can imagine what is going on: hundreds of men drilling on the parade ground, four-mule teams and motor trucks hauling supplies, and one thing I nearly forgot was that one can look up and see army aeroplanes sailing about most any time. Every man, animal, and machine is doing its duty in a businesslike manner and no one is seen loafing around.

The main part of this camp or the business center is the
Quarter-master Department. This is made up of about twenty-
five large buildings where all the supplies are received and
then issued out to each regiment. It is here where you may
see numbers of four-mule teams and trucks coming in each
morning to receive their rations. Then they are hauled to the
different regiments. It is common, even, to see twenty-four-
mule teams hauling their loads of supplies away. They look
mighty fine all in one string and it means a lot of stuff, too.
You know they take real loads on these army wagons.[8]

Camp MacArthur was still under construction when the boys
arrived—in particular, the airfield, hangars, and barracks. Wilbert
Murphy, who wrote his letter from the local YMCA, expected the
camp to ultimately hold fifty thousand men or more—the entire
National Guard from both Wisconsin and Michigan in addition
to many drafted men from Michigan. He and others described the
creation of the 32nd Division from the Wisconsin and Michigan

Soldiers gather at the YMCA game room at Camp MacArthur in Waco,
Texas, ca. 1917. WHI IMAGE ID 74802

National Guard units. The Wisconsin infantry regiments became the 127th and 128th Infantry Regiments and the 121st Machine Gun Battalion. Murphy went into Company M, 128th Infantry.[9]

Reuel Barlow went with the field hospital of the 127th Infantry; on the side, he wrote for the *Madison Democrat*. He also wrote a long letter to his friend and editor of the *Monticello Messenger* describing Texas and life at Camp MacArthur.

Hello Earle: Doubtless a few lines from the Sunny Southland when Wisconsin folks are experiencing snow and ice, and from an army camp in these patriotic times, will not be amiss. For ideal weather at this time of the year, I do not see how Texas could be beat. I am sitting with sleeves rolled up and shirt open at the collar. Our tent is thrown partly back so that I can almost look straight up at the moon and stars. There is just the slightest touch of coolness in the air; enough to make one feel like a million dollars. The days are anywhere from mildly warm to hot. We have had one cool morning, when a "norther" blew down upon us from somewhere up north, and it seemed to me that I could smell good old Wisconsin air in that wind.

Every Wisconsin soldier here notices one thing. That is, the scarcity of trees and the flat country. As a result the wind gets a good sweep and we have had a couple of gales here that were worse than a blizzard, for the air becomes full of fine, black, gumbo dust and objects a hundred yards away cannot be seen. When a storm starts in, we shut everything up tight, even our eyes and mouths. One day last week we were all kept inside nearly all day, and before noon we all looked like the coal man—eyebrows all black, nose black, mouth and ears black. Luckily, storms of this kind don't happen every day.

Cotton is growing on all sides of us here, and it is being picked as fast as it is ready. Horned toads, lizards, mistletoe

growing on the trees, and buzzards, sometimes a dozen
sitting in one tree, are some of the things to be found here.
Downtown in the city of Waco, is an interesting sight. The
court-house square is the oldest part of town. It reminds one
of pictures of Old Mexico. Negroes, hundreds of them, Mex-
icans sitting flat on the sidewalk with their backs against the
walls of the buildings, a few Chinamen and Italians, cowboys
and soldiers make an unusual sight. The main part of the business section looks like any city with its large show windows
and electric lights. Negroes there are scarce and that is where
the soldiers go when they are in town.

The people here are almost too hospitable. On the streetcars and on the street, they invite you to something, either
church, a social, or to dinner. Two fellows in our tent refused
an offer last Sunday to ride in an auto to one man's home for
dinner, and they were almost mobbed when they came back
to camp. The white people here have fine homes and they
know how to enjoy them.

Every man in our company is feeling like a top. Edwin
Barlow [Reuel's cousin] will have to be careful or he will have
a double chin. I have taken on eight pounds in weight and
one of our cooks has jumped from 140 to 187 pounds during
the last fifteen weeks. Some of the fat fellows have worked
down so that they look like the rest of us now. Our work is
not hard. We hike four miles after breakfast, have an hour of
physical exercise, and then drill. In the afternoon we have lectures and studies for about two hours. On Saturdays we hike
from ten to twelve miles in the morning.

Tomorrow (Sunday) morning is inspection. My shoes are
shined, whiskers cut off and hair cut; and my shirt, breeches
and leggings are scrubbed absolutely clean. They must not
have a spot on them. That is the way in the army. Our teeth
and finger nails even are inspected, and we must show clean

underwear, socks, towel, comb, tooth-brush and soap case, besides a lot of other equipment.

We now have wooden floors, wooden sidewalks, iron beds with springs in them, electric lights and stoves in our tents. The stoves will probably come in very nice before next month is by.

I can hear a couple bands playing, several musical instruments nearby, a quartette in the next tent singing something about "Getting the Kaiser," and a couple dozen mules braying, grunting and snorting in the big corral where several thousand are kept. We play football and basketball, get a chicken dinner once in a while and plenty of sweet potatoes that are as yellow as pumpkins, so we are all enjoying ourselves.[10]

In mid-November, Wilbert Murphy wrote to describe the progress of the training.

This week has been the busiest or one of the busiest we have had. Two days were spent on the range digging trenches and constructing fortifications to practice on. The trenches are watched closely and no one except the soldiers is allowed to be in or around them. No one is permitted to take any pictures of them. We expect to live in them before long so we are making the best of our time to get instruction about them. Night work began this week. It is also very secret and is carried out under the most rigid discipline. No one is permitted to talk and orders are given in a whisper. It is interesting dope and is practically similar to campaign conditions.

This morning we took a hike lasting about three hours. Most of us wore our new hiking shoes, so when we got back, our feet were rather sore. We have been issued more shoes which are to be worn on hikes, and in the trenches. They are made of unpolished leather, have soles about half inch in thickness and an iron plate on the heel and hob nails in the soles. They are built to last and I don't think a person can ever wear them out.

Our 32nd Division Foot Ball team played the Second Texas team at the Cotton Palace Exposition this afternoon. Some of the fellows went, but the rain stopped a lot from going. We won 22 to 0.

The fellows are all well and I think they are enjoying themselves. We are getting into the real work now. If things in Europe go on as they have for the past few months, we may take the trip across the "pond." Some French officers are at this camp now instructing us in modern methods. They have seen service in several of the important battles and give some interesting lectures covering their experiences.[11]

Training at Camp MacArthur also included dealing with the deadly gases that were used for the first time in World War I.

Training included learning to use gas masks. Both men and horses were equipped to use them. WHI IMAGE ID 113136

Charles Marshall, who was also with the 127th Field Hospital, wrote:

> We are beginning to realize more and more that we are into something, and we haven't even been "over there." We went through two kinds of gas tests last week. Tear gas, which we go through without masks, sure makes you cry some, and then chlorine gas which we go through with gas masks. The latter tests we have been having for quite a while; the masks protect you entirely from it. One of the English non-coms said that the Germans started the gas, but that the Allies had, at present, by far the most dangerous gases, and that the Huns wish they had never begun using it.[12]

At least one of the Green County boys died at Camp Mac-Arthur. The front page of the *Brooklyn Teller* in early December proclaimed, "Ben Johnson Is Victim of Pneumonia." Johnson had enlisted in April with his brother Einar and several other Brooklyn boys. They were all members of Company M with the 128th Infantry. "News of the death of Private Ben Johnson, which occurred in the base hospital at Camp MacArthur, Waco, Texas, came as a distinct shock to relatives and friends in this village and vicinity."[13]

CAMP MERRITT AND NEW YORK CITY

During January and February 1918, the troops of the 32nd Division left Camp MacArthur for Camp Merritt, New Jersey, to await their transport across the Atlantic from the port at Hoboken. Camp Merritt was called a "rest camp." One Brod-head boy remarked that the name was appropriate "as we do nothing at all but sleep and eat, except a little hike in the a.m. and guard duty."[14]

Many of the boys took advantage of the opportunity to see
New York City. Elmer Swann wrote home to his family about
the experience:

> We saw the City yesterday; we got around and among sub-
> ways and elevated cars as though we'd lived here forever. We
> landed for our first stop on 42nd and Broadway, from which
> place we saw the Times buildings and the Astor Hotel in the
> theatre part of the city.
>
> Then we hit a subway down to Woolworth's building
> where we went to its top by elevator. Spread out before us was
> the harbor of New York and main business section of the larg-
> est city in the world. You can imagine we were in a position to
> see the place almost as well as if we had been in an airplane;
> we were almost 800 feet high. Close around the building we
> were on were the skyscrapers of the city: the Singer Building,
> the Times Tower, the Flatiron, and others of note. Looking
> out into the misty harbor we could see the Goddess of Lib-
> erty, Brooklyn and Manhattan bridges, Manhattan, Brooklyn,
> Staten and Ellis Islands.
>
> After we descended the building, or, I should say the ele-
> vator descended us, we lunched and went down to the water
> front passing through Wall Street and the Stock Exchange.
> Down on the wharfs we saw the Aquarium, the Customs
> House, and numerous passenger and freight boats scurrying
> and dodging each other in the harbor like autos on a crowded
> street.
>
> After a rest and supper at the Algonquin Hotel, we took
> in the New York Hippodrome Theatre. Wish you could have
> been with us yesterday because I know you would all have
> enjoyed it just as much as I.[15]

Theodore Roosevelt came to Camp Merritt on January 30 to dedicate Merritt Hall, a club for the common soldier. Elmer Swann also described this experience:

> Teddy Roosevelt gave us a dandy talk. Although the camp auditorium is very large, it couldn't begin to hold the eager crowd of men; so, many resorted to beams and rafters. Teddy was the same as you see of him in papers and pictures. He certainly did roast the Germans. He said that although we had a hard, dangerous piece of work before us, that we were an army to be envied because we were going to thrash the Kaiser and his Hunnish followers. The fellows just simply went wild.[16]

CHAPTER TWO

~

To France

By the time Roosevelt spoke at Camp Merritt, at the end of January 1918, the advance detachment of the 32nd Division had already arrived at Brest, France. It took some time to move the twenty-seven thousand troops, nine thousand horses and mules, motor cars, trucks, artillery, and equipment from Camp Mac-Arthur to Camp Merritt. Before all had arrived to Camp Merritt, others had crossed the ocean. The 32nd was the sixth US division to arrive in France. It was not until mid-May 1918 that it would be assigned to frontline duty. Until then, the men would get acquainted with France.[1]

THE TRIP ACROSS THE POND

The 32nd suffered its first casualties during the passage to France. Some of the men were aboard the SS *Tuscania* bound for Liverpool, England, when it was torpedoed and sunk by a German submarine off the coast of northern Ireland, on the evening of February 5. More than 2,000 American troops were aboard this luxury liner, and some 210 men died in the attack, including 13 men from the 32nd Division. It was the first ship carrying American troops to be sunk.[2]

Family and friends back in Green County, Wisconsin, were understandably nervous as the rest of the 32nd Division troops made the trip during late February and early March. On March 13, 1918, the *Brooklyn Teller* proclaimed, "Brooklyn Soldiers Safely Across." The brief article read, "There has been great rejoicing in this community since it was learned that the contingent of troops, which included a number of Brooklyn boys, had reached France in safety the middle of last week. The news brought with it great relief, as the recent *Tuscania* disaster increased the misgivings of parents, other relatives, and friends."[3]

During much of April and May, the newspapers printed news and letters from the boys announcing their safe arrival and telling a bit about the trip over. Einar Johnson and Otis O'Brien of Brooklyn wrote to describe their trip across. According to the editor, the boys were both "employed as waiters in the officers' mess and had an opportunity to view more of the scenery on the voyage than many of the others. A submarine was encountered, but the American gunners kept it so busy, there was no time to let loose a torpedo. All hands were on deck during the encounter, cheering like a bunch of college boys at a football game."[4] Fred Amstutz of Monticello wrote, "We sure had some trip across. There wasn't many of the boys sick. I was somewhat sick the day we went aboard ship, but was all O.K. again the third day out. We had the honor of riding on one of the largest ships in the world. There was plenty of entertainment, with music and moving pictures in our mess hall every night."[5]

Clarence Bontly, also of Monticello, was thrilled with the trip across; he wrote:

> First of all, I want to tell you of our trip across. It was simply great, and I have never enjoyed anything quite so much. Sergeant McClure and I had a state room together, while the rest

of the boys had to sleep down in the hole and had but two
meals a day. We had our three meals a day, so you can see how
lucky we were.

While we were in the danger zone we had but two meals
and a light lunch. But we were never in any danger. The nearest thing to a sub we saw was a school of sharks. We had fine
weather and none of us were seasick.[6]

Others were seasick and enjoyed the trip less. Melvin Lynn
later recalled how "old Cedric steamed out of the New York harbor and into the black waters of the Atlantic, and how the people
on the ferry boats cheered us. There were many seasick days and
nights passed on board. At night not a light was to be seen and
the thought that we might encounter a sub, at almost any time,
sure gave one a creepy feeling. But after having been on the water
a few days we forgot all about the subs and devoted our time to
feeding the fish."[7]

Wilbert Murphy was among those who enjoyed the fourteen
days spent crossing the Atlantic, and he was particularly impressed with the harbor at Brest, France. "Here was certainly a
sight worth seeing. The harbor was chocked with shipping, big
boats and smaller craft, submarines, destroyers, and the like. It
was a great sight to us and we were on deck most of the time
watching the movements of the boats."[8]

FIRST IMPRESSIONS OF FRANCE

For most of the boys, however, their impressions of the trip across
were soon overwhelmed by their activity after arrival and their
initial impressions of France. Since none of the American troops
saw major action at the front until May, the early letters from the
boys of the 32nd reflected a mix of uncertainty and apprehension

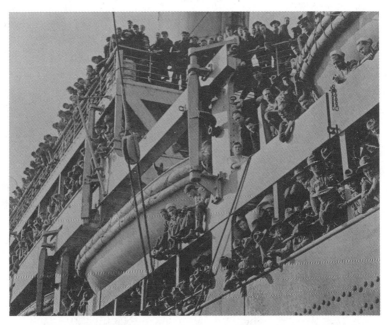

The men of the 32nd Division traveled across the ocean on various transport ships in early 1918. Many of them arrived at Brest, France, as did these men aboard the steamship *Leviathan*. WHI IMAGE ID 132644

about the job ahead of them, with a heavy dose of curiosity about this strange new land. This letter from Otis O'Brien to his mother back in the Brooklyn area is a good example. It was dated March 17, 1918, "Somewhere in France."

Dear Mother,

Well at last we have reached our new home, and it was a tiresome ride across France in those crowded trains. We were camped near the coast for twenty-four hours and then came here. We were on the train three days and were so crowded we could not lie down at all, so we were pretty tired when we reached this place.

We are in a small town and live in billets or barns, old houses, etc. I am quartered in a hay mow. There are about twenty of us up there and it is so dark at all times we have to remember where we put our belongings if we want to find them again. All the buildings are of stone here, even the roofs, and everybody has a stone fence around his property.

It is real spring and all the gardens are planted, and what men there are left are working in the fields. It sure is a strange country without any young men around at all. Everybody seems to be at the front.

I wish I could take pictures around here. Some of the sights you have to see them to believe them. An old fellow, who seems to be the village newspaper, comes around every day with a drum and when he gets the people out to listen, he reads the news to them. When they use two, three, or four horses, they hitch them up one ahead of the other. Almost every morning you can see a door open and a bunch of chickens and geese come out and then four or five cows, and then a bunch of soldiers. They seem to have house and barn all in one building.

Firewood is the scarcest article over here, and about all there is left to burn now is brush.

They say we can hear the big guns on the front from here; but there does not seem to be much excitement around. From the reports we get here the Germans cannot figure out the U.S. soldiers because they go at it like they mean business.

Hoping we will soon be home again and back to civilization, and with love to all,

Otis O'Brien[9]

The French trains that O'Brien briefly mentioned greeted almost all the infantrymen. One described them this way: "The French train is not like one in the U.S. Our train was made up of about 35 box cars which are about one-half the size of a box car at home. They are marked '8 *chevaux ou 40 hommes*' which in English is 'eight horses or forty men.' You have a little straw on the floor of the car with which to make your bed."[10]

Charles Marshall, from the Brodhead area, undoubtedly had a similar train ride before he was settled enough to write a first letter from the Camp Hospital Headquarters of the 32nd Division:

> Well, I'm here at last. I can't tell you exactly where, but will as soon as we get the Kaiser licked. We had quite a trip over and landed safely. I saw in thirty minutes after I landed a lot of things I never saw before. Things sure are funny over here, the wagons, railroads, etc. You will see a couple of Tommies [British soldiers] on an Irish cart, behind a mule, an engine that is a joke compared to ours, and many other queer and interesting things. However, when you see this country you know what war means. The people are so much in earnest, you see all men, young and old, in uniform; and now we know what we are fighting for.[11]

Many of the boys, like Wilbert Murphy, were quickly intrigued by the French and eager to learn their language:

> Finally we are just about settled enough so at least I have time enough to write to you. I'm picking up a little French, before long I hope to be able to talk it. We are quartered in a little village somewhere in France. The houses are all stone buildings, by the way we don't all sleep in houses either—some of us get barns. We are comfortably situated though and will like it better as we get accustomed to it.
>
> Had a fine trip across. The weather was splendid, and I didn't get sea sick. The first night over here we slept in one of Napoleon's old camps, prisons I think.

When the American troops first arrived in France, they often stayed in old stone farmhouses and barns. WHI IMAGE ID 132652

French people seem rather strange with their language and their wooden shoes but I think when we have been here longer and have learned their language and customs we won't think them so queer. There is an old bachelor in the house where I am billeted, and he surely is a fine old man. He gave us a lantern and lets us use some of his pans to wash in.[12]

When Reuel Barlow wrote home to his father on March 18, he commented on the beautiful spring weather and the fact that the grass was green and vegetable gardens were growing. "The country here looks like Wisconsin, but the fields are not bigger than good-sized gardens and each field is enclosed by a hedge, instead of a fence." He also noted that the women were all dressed in black.[13]

A couple of weeks later, when he was more settled, Barlow wrote to his brother:

> I am well and quite happy. We are running a camp hospital similar to the one at Camp Douglas, only in barracks. Everything is quite comfortable, except for the mud, as we are getting lots of rain. There are scores of springs around here, some no doubt that are permanent, but many due to the heavy rains. The trees are turning green. I have picked blue and white violets and the French dandelions are out, also jonquils and several other kinds of flowers.
>
> We can get some good feeds here in the French villages. The other evening we jaunted for half an hour to town, passing the home of a count who is at the front. I ate four fried eggs, rye bread, a plate heaped full of French fried potatoes, jam, cheese and half a quart bottle of wine. The entire meal cost me 3.75 francs, or about 68 cents. We ate in the kitchen and the two French women who live there prepared our meal. They have several children and their husbands are in the army. We talked to them in French, and they would hardly believe some of the things we told them about America.

One thing Barlow missed, however, was reading material. "What I want is good magazines. If you can get any, send them along. If I don't get a little reading, I will take to writing poetry, and that would be awful."[14]

About a month later when he wrote to his father on May 1, Barlow was still working in the office of the camp hospital and had recently been made corporal. He was also still enjoying the food and the people. He and his cousin Edwin had befriended a French family:

They invite us over a couple times a week. They cannot speak English, but we can speak French well enough to get along pretty well, and we have some pretty good cake and wine at their house. We gave the man the tobacco one night, and he grabbed Edwin around the shoulders and kissed him because he had given him an unusually large amount. They have a daughter about fourteen years old, and she is learning English at school. We have lots of fun speaking to her in English.[15]

Elmer Swann of Brodhead wrote several letters home between the end of March and early May.[16] Like others, he was struck by the beauty of the French countryside and the high quality of their roads. He marveled at the "rolling hills whose sides are covered checkered with small (acre) plots of ground, surrounded by zig-zag thorny hedges." He continued, "Little rivulets and creeks, gurgling down the rock ledges and craggy hills, can be heard almost anywhere one goes. The climate is refreshing and appetizing to say the least."

He noted the "interesting old castles and Roman amphitheaters built back in Caesar's time" and remarked on "the conscientious way in which they were built [to] have stood the decay of hundreds of years remarkably well." He was glad to have studied some history.

Swann was involved with hospital work and was billeted in an old château "of the old French style; stone walls, tile roof, steel barred windows which can be covered with heavy wooden shutters." At this point they were well back from the action at the front: "Although we aren't on the front lines, we are coming more and more to see purpose in all our preparation. That purpose used to seem vague and far away, but now it's becoming more real every day, as we hear what sounds to me like the roar of heavy guns on clear evenings when the wind is just right."

Like Barlow, Swann was enjoying the French people and their food. He told the following story of one night's experience:

Two of us are looking after a company of our soldiers who are billeted in a little peasant village, and we also take care of civilians who highly appreciate a favor. Last night we bandaged a little boy's knee, skinned by falling down. He was much afraid of us when he found out we were going to bandage his leg. But after his uncle explained that it wouldn't hurt at all, he submitted like a regular gentleman. The boy's folks immediately called us in for a glass of France's favorite wine. After drinking it, we had a very enjoyable and instructive conversation, they learning English and we French.

He continued,

I am getting so that I understand considerable French if they don't talk too fast, and can talk quite a bit myself. We find the best way to learn French and at the same time have a good time and mingle with the people is to eat a dinner or supper with a family. They bring out all we can eat of very well cooked food, way ahead of an army meal. They seem to have as good a time as we do. Here is what we had for supper one evening with a French family: Rich thick soup, four eggs a piece, fried roast pork, cucumber pickles, string beans (last year's), bread, red wine, chocolate pudding, French cookies, and a good night drink of some sort (not alcoholic). The red wine is diluted and drunk as we would tea or coffee. They filled our glasses as often and as soon as emptied. Bread from a big loaf was cut and passed around by the Mr. as soon as what we had was gone.

Swann's father, back home in Wisconsin, had planted wheat that year. The US government was urging farmers to plant wheat for the war effort, since many of the French fields could not be farmed. Wrote Swann:

> It's fine that Dad has put in so much wheat this year, because it is going to be high this fall. The United States is lucky that she has plenty of man power to work her vast acres. Here in France you can see very few men working in the fields. There are eight or ten women to every man. They don't seem to take it so very hard either. The French have their faults: are given to going to extremes, very passionate, but they have a pretty solid reserve. They are very friendly to me and we get along with them fine.

Uncle Sam was also pleading with American consumers to conserve food for the war effort and observe "meatless days" and "wheatless days." Requartte Hahn, who was also a farmboy, had not noticed any shortages of food for the troops:

> I don't see how anyone could make out that we are not getting sugar, butter, and white bread. I'll guarantee that we are just as near the head end as others and we get all the sugar we want, either butter or jam each meal and good white bread. Why honestly I don't see where that could be unless in England, because this army is sure treating us fine as far as food is concerned. For breakfast we have eggs and potatoes or cornmeal mush and milk and sugar, or bacon and fried potatoes or bacon and pancakes, combined with coffee and bread and syrup. Then for dinner we generally have roast beef or beef stew with potatoes and some kind of side dish, like bread pudding or peaches or prunes and bread and butter and tea.

For supper we have sometimes steaks or hamburger with potatoes and bread, butter and jam. Who would kick about that? I'm mighty sure I don't.[17]

Like the other boys, Hahn was enjoying the people and places of France. He wrote of riding horseback for about fifteen miles through the countryside. "We had a mighty fine trip. It is certainly wonderful all the experiences a soldier can have at this time. I never dreamed of such things. Imagine me, Dad and Mother, riding about France on horseback!" Along the road:

> We came to an old stone house and stopped to rest. Well, we went in the house. It didn't look like anyone lived there when we first arrived, but they were home and we went right in and they made us right to home. They had a little baby about a year and one half old I guess, and I wish you could have heard her talk. She would say "wee" in the cutest little way you ever heard. I believe that was the first time I ever enjoyed having a baby around. Well the Madam scrambled eggs for us, and we had bread and butter and cider. A fine little feed. When we went to go, she absolutely refused to take a cent and acted hurt because we offered it to her. Well we gave the baby ten francs between us and left. That is just the way most of the people around here are.[18]

ON NEWS FROM HOME

One thing that appeared in almost every letter was mention of the mail: whether they had been receiving mail and how much it meant to them. Hahn had begun the above-mentioned letter, written in May 1918, exactly that way:

When the men had free time, they spent much of it writing letters home.
WHI IMAGE ID 88625

"Dear Folks—I received some more large envelopes from you yesterday. There were three different letters in them and they were all mighty fine letters too. I sure do enjoy getting letters over here. I could just sit and read them for hours at a time. I suppose it is because they are such a long ways apart, not so long at that, only a week or so, but it seems about a year when a fellow is waiting to hear from home.[19]

Some of the mail might contain candy, tobacco, or other items from home; sometimes it arrived safely and other times it did not. Hahn continued that one "envelope was torn at one end showing just where the tobacco had gotten out. But you don't need to worry about me getting tobacco and candy over here. We get a regular issue of tobacco now; and as to candy, well a fellow can't expect to have everything here that he had at home. You must never worry for one minute about me because I am getting along just fine."[20]

The hometown newspaper editors also sent newspapers over-sees to the boys. Reuel Barlow wrote to his friend at the *Monticello Messenger*.

> I want to write a few lines to let you know that the home folks
> and friends and the home paper are very much in our minds
> away over here, and that they stand out as the strong tie that
> binds us to the good old United States. I want to emphasize
> [this] with all sincerity. Over here war news is not half as in-
> teresting as home news. The Paris papers we read quickly and
> then throw them away, while a copy of the *Messenger* we keep
> for several days, or until we read every line of it.[21]

Through the hometown newspapers the boys could also read each other's letters recounting experiences at the front.

Of course the business of writing letters home was compli-cated by the fact that the mail was censored to screen out any information that might help the enemy. Some were frustrated by this, and, like Wilbert Murphy, were discouraged from writing. For example, he wrote: "Some more mail came for me today and I'm surely ashamed of myself for not writing sooner and oftener. I realize you are anxious, but there is so very little to write that we can tell. Did I ever tell you about the French towns? I guess I did, but will tell you again anyway." Murphy closed this letter with a touching assurance of his sincerity: "I never knew what home was till I got over here; and I never knew or at least didn't realize how good my dear old dad and mother were to me. With lots of love, Your son, Wilbert."[22]

CHAPTER THREE

At the Front

The record of the 32nd Division at the front was one of considerable achievement, but it began with great disappointment, particularly for many of the Wisconsin troops. General Pershing had decided that the sixth division to arrive in France would serve to provide replacement troops wherever they were needed. That happened to be the 32nd Division. Although Pershing was eventually persuaded that the 32nd could be more valuable if left

intact, that was only after some seven thousand Wisconsin infantrymen were transferred to the First Division to fill in for the casualties.

Thus, the Wisconsin infantrymen of the 32nd Division who trained at Waco together had a

Men of the 32nd Division stand at the ready in the trenches.
WHI IMAGE ID 112963

divided experience at the front. Nearly half of them—the privates and captains in the 128th Infantry—went as replacement troops into the First Division; and the other half—the 127th Infantry—stayed with the 32nd Division. Many of those who left were cheered at the thought that they would see action sooner, but it was nevertheless a difficult blow not to be serving together.[1]

WISCONSIN BOYS JOIN
THE FIRST DIVISION

Wilbert Murphy had not yet been at the front line when he wrote to his folks on May 4, but he was headed that way. Murphy was among those reassigned to the First Division; he shifted to Company D of the 28th Infantry.

The First Division belonged to the regular army. It was the first American division in France and had begun to arrive in mid-June 1917. It had entered the line in relatively quiet sectors for instructional purposes in the fall of 1917, but it wasn't until April 1918 that it embarked on its first important task at the village of Cantigny, about one hundred or so kilometers north of Paris. Wilbert Murphy moved with the First Division for that effort.

By May 7 he was close enough to the frontline trenches to have spoken with troops that had just come out of them.

I was talking to a fellow that had been in the trenches and he said that I'd have a lot of new experiences when I got up there. He has been up twice and says he feels as though he had his share. You know the Boche use a lot of gas on us. Well, every night, after you have crawled down in your dugout to sleep, he opens up on you and cheats you out of your sleep. When you are wearing a gas mask, it is hard to sleep. That may sound like the "square heads" make it miserable for us, but for every shell he sends at us, we give him a dozen at least.

Soldiers had to buy their own life insurance in World War I. Murphy had mentioned it in a previous letter, and he brought it up again in this one. He was already having money taken out of his wages to buy a Liberty Bond. "When I get the Liberty Bond paid for I will have an allotment taken out to be sent to you. The Liberty Bond takes $10 a month now, so when it is paid I can take out a $10 or $15 allotment. The insurance takes $6.40 a month, but it is worth it, for you will get $57.50 per month for twenty years if I get bumped off here (which I don't expect will happen)."[2]

Most of the Brooklyn boys were also transferred to the First Division. The *Brooklyn Teller* had reported the news of the breakup of Company M on May 1. Otis O'Brien and Einar Johnson had both written letters home telling what happened. Johnson's letter had been considerably censored, but the paper printed this excerpt: "The company was split up last Friday. The captain and all the privates left for [censored] and all the corporals and sergeants were left here. I had just made corporal so I couldn't go. Tried to, but there was no chance. It was hard to see the fellows leave, and I wish I could see some fighting too. They say we are going to stay here and drill other companies."[3]

Private Otis O'Brien took advantage of the opportunity to volunteer with a motor supply company. As a farmboy from a prosperous dairy county, he had experience with engines and automobiles. In an earlier letter he'd remarked on the fact that his brother Lyle was making good with the 20th Engineers. They had been impressed with his experience in steam engines. Wrote O'Brien, "I wish I could have known they wanted steam engineers before we left the States."[4]

By May 6, when he wrote the following letter from "Somewhere in France," O'Brien was driving a truck with a First Division supply train. (He, like Murphy, would also have been in northern France for the Cantigny effort.) O'Brien wrote vivid descriptions of his activities, despite the threat of censorship:

Dear Mother,

When I write that "Somewhere in France," I wish I could tell you more about our location. It is sure a lively place on this front, and the boys are laying 'em over tonight. They started about five o'clock, and it has been a steady roar ever since.

The Boche got wise to our supply depot and started over to bomb it last Friday while all our trucks were there. The artillery held them off for a while; and while we were watching it, there appeared fifty French aeroplanes so quick that the eight Boche planes beat it. The Frenchmen went right on over the lines after them; I think they showed the Boche they could drop bombs too. I saw in the paper the next day where eight German planes were shot down, and several tons of bombs were dropped.

Last night I saw a sight which I had never dreamed of before. I was up on the front among our artillery and watched "no man's land" after dark. We were up on a hill so we could see both the Boche and American lines. Rockets of all colors were in the air all the time. They also keep the air full of star shells which make it just as light as day. The Boche were not sending over very many shells, but we could see one of them burst now and then.

We cannot go up to the front during the day because the Boche can see a truck pretty easy and they have a habit of shelling the roads. We could not go up the road another quarter of a mile to turn around last night because they had been shelling the road. It is some job to turn around a bunch of trucks on that narrow road in the dark, too.

Today is our day of rest. We get about every sixth day off to clean up our trucks, and we have inspection and about two hours drill. The last few days are enough to give one the spring fever, and everyone is talking about fishing. I suppose they are biting good out in King Lake about now.

You should have seen the feed we had for dinner. We had steak, mashed potatoes, gravy, cauliflower, radishes, and coffee. We are on French rations now so we started a mess fund. Most of the boys donated five or ten francs and we have a good sized fund started now. We get more good out of a few francs that way because the French cafés sure do hold us up for a feed. [The American boys bought and cooked additional food, rather than visiting the expensive French cafés.]

A family of refugees passed thru here the other day. I did not think that the Germans treated the people like the papers said they did, but I believe it now. There was a man and his wife and three or four children. The oldest of these was a girl about eight years old; and the Boche had cut off part of her right foot to cripple her. The man was all cuts and scars inflicted by them, too. They were the nearest to starving of anything I had ever seen. The troops gave them all the food they could carry and also took up a collection of money for them.

Guess I must be wound up tonight or else the sound of the guns affects me. This is some letter for me, don't you think? I hope this finds everybody well and happy. Who is driving the car now, Wilma or dad? Well, write and let me know how everything is getting along.

As ever, with lots of love,

Otis[5]

Thorwald and Bernie Christensen, also from Brooklyn, were separated when the 128th Infantry broke up. Bernie "happened to be in the hospital" when the split occurred, so he stayed with the 32nd Division in the training area.[6] Thorwald went with the First Division to northern France; when he wrote home on May 31, he gave few details: "Well, Mother, I have been over the top and came out of it without a scratch. Am feeling fine, but would like a little more mail."[7] He was similarly vague when he wrote again on July 26. "Well, Mom, I've had all kinds of war lately. I was over the top three times in five days and didn't get so much as a scratch. We drove the Huns back about [censored] kilometers. Melvin Berger, the lad that used to be with Ben Johnson and me so much, got a slight wound in the leg; he will get over it in a week or so, I think."[8]

Bernie, however, had not yet seen the kind of action his brother had when he wrote on July 5. He wrote a lighthearted letter about losing "boko francs" in a craps game and about his job delivering messages. He continued, "Say, do you know that I think I could stick to a job better than before I enlisted. I have held this job in the army longer than any place I ever worked. They don't seem to want to fire a guy here."[9]

IN AND OUT OF THE TRENCHES
WITH THE 32ND

After spending several weeks training and engaged in construction work on supply depots, the 32nd Division moved to the front in mid-May. Beginning May 18 until July 21, the 32nd held the front in the quiet sector of Alsace. There the 32nd Division troops had the distinction of being the first Americans to set foot on German soil; Alsace was a historically contested area between the Germans and French. But because it was a quiet sector, the division was still assembling itself during that time. It received replacements for the men that had gone to join the First Division, and it completed its training. In early July 1918, Pershing inspected the division and liked what he saw. The commanding officer, General Haan, was eager to move to an active front. Pershing is reported to have told him, "I like the snap in your division, and unless I am mistaken, you will be on your way to a more active front in the very near future. Tell your men I like their spirit."[10]

The men of the 32nd Division are the first American troops to set foot on German soil, in Alsace. The pole near the center of the picture marks the 1914 boundary between France and Germany. THE WISCONSIN VETERANS MUSEUM (MADISON, WI)

Thus when Sergeant Fred Amstutz from Monticello wrote to his sister right before the Fourth of July, he had just undergone an initial tour in the trenches; but he experienced more rats than combat:

> We just got back from the trenches and are all cleaned up for the Fourth. No place to celebrate, however. We are in a small village and they don't seem to understand that it is our national independence day.
>
> Well, our company was in the trenches for [censored] nights and [censored] days. It sure was sport for us. The first night I was in charge of the munitions. I would make the rounds about once every hour and every time I went out through the trenches I would hear a few rats, and I thought there was a Boche around. I would walk a few steps and stop, and I'll admit there was a funny sensation playing up and

down my spinal column. But I soon got over it. I finally came to relieve another sergeant and I got some laughs from the privates who had been in the trenches for [censored] days.

I was out on a patrol one night and it put me in mind of hunting rabbits. We'd go sneaking along with our pistols in our hands, always on the lookout for "big game." Why, it isn't half bad. But you think we have rats in the States. The rats are as thick, over here, as cats and dogs are at home. At night the rats run in the wire and sometimes we think the Boches are coming, so we throw over a hand grenade merely to play safe.[11]

Less than three weeks later, Fred Amstutz was the first Monticello boy to be killed in action. Both he and his brother Sam fought with Company H of the 127th Infantry; Sam was wounded at the same time Fred was killed, on July 24. The *Monticello Messenger* reported Fred's death at the end of August.[12]

It surely made a difference for the boys to spend relatively quiet time in the trenches before moving to more active fronts.

They needed some time to get used to the conditions—including the rats. When Elmer Swann of Brodhead wrote from the Alsace trenches on July 9, like Amstutz, he commented on the rats. (Swann was with the field hospital of the 127th Infantry. The hospital moved with the 127th.)

Sergeant Fred Amstutz was the first WWI soldier from Monticello to be killed in battle. *MONTICELLO MESSENGER,* SEPT. 11, 1918

As to the way we spend our evenings, after we go inside, we
write letters, tell stories, discuss the events of the day, specu-
late on how long the war will last, smoke a little, make French
toast from stuff we have begged from the kitchen and devour
a can of pears or peaches that we have purchased in a nearby
Y.M.C.A. the previous day. Being dark in our military cellars
(dugouts) and away from the roar of the heavy guns, it is a
fairly good place to sleep. When you lie down though, the
only way to do so is to commend yourself to the care of the
rats and your imagination. In this way you'll surely sleep very
soundly. One night while I was slumbering, a big rat jumped
off a shelf above my bed, down onto my face, then down to
the floor. Judging from the looks of my physog [face] the next
morning, Mr. Rat must have been wearing hob-nails. But
you mustn't think that there are rats in every dugout, because
there aren't. Now if we should go into a place minus rats we
should be happily disappointed.[13]

The tone of the boys' letters changed markedly once they
reached the front lines of an active sector. Reuel Barlow of Monticello wrote to his sister at the end of July, "We are in the thick
of the fight and are not green at this business any more. Have
seen things that would make you throw up your Thanksgiving
dinner—dead Germans and parts of them, anything you want
to imagine." In another letter to his father written about the same
time, Barlow said that he had just seen both of the Amstutz boys
a few days previously. Barlow's letters were published alongside
the articles announcing the death of Sergeant Fred Amstutz.[14]

The tone of Bernie Christensen's letters had also changed
markedly by the time he wrote to his mother on August 4:

We had some time yesterday, but I pulled out without a
scratch, so guess I am pretty lucky. Would like to tell you all

The 32nd Division captured the important town of Fismes, pictured here in early August 1918. WHI IMAGE ID 131013

about it but can't; will tell you everything when I get home. Don't worry about me if I don't write so often, Mother, because once in a while we don't have time.

I can't help but think of the nice places at home when we go into towns that the Germans have shot all to pieces and ruined. When you see things like that it makes your blood boil. You have seen pictures in the magazines of places all blown up; I used to think they stretched it, but they aren't painted bad enough.[15]

In the same column of the *Brooklyn Teller* were several other letters from Brooklyn boys fighting with the 32nd Division. Two of these letters were from Einar Johnson. Johnson was the one who had just made corporal and thus stayed with Company M and the 128th Infantry, when the other Brooklyn boys were sent to the First Division. He wrote to his mother on August 5.

Haven't been able to write before because we have been in
the big drive. We have been after the Boche night and day,
our division driving them farther than any of the others did.
It is open warfare here, but we have them almost back to the
trenches again.

The first morning we went in, we drove them out of a
little village and kept them on the go for two days before
they stopped for real battle. We were under fire of the big
guns one afternoon and a night. It was pretty exciting and
at first it made me wish I was home, but the Germans didn't
hold out long.

We were relieved that morning and before night the other
bunch had them five kilometers over the river. Guess we must
have driven them all of ten miles.

The Boche are a bunch of cowards. They will fight until
one is almost to them and then they will holler, "Kamerad."
They can't stop the Americans. If we keep them going the way
they are now, we will soon have them in Berlin.[16]

About ten days later Johnson wrote home again, this time to
his father:

I suppose you have seen in the paper that we are in the big
American drive. We have been in some of the real dope and
seen quite a little fighting. Our division drove the Boche
[censored] kilometers. The night before we were relieved we
laid in a German barrage all night. Those big shells sure did
whistle all around us but nobody was hurt. We camped one
night near Lieut Quentin Roosevelt's grave. [Quentin, the
youngest son of Theodore Roosevelt, was a pilot with the
95th Aero Squadron. He was shot down July 12, 1918, at the
age of twenty.] I got a rivet out of his machine for a souvenir.

I have seen Lyle [O'Brien] and Arnold [Hansen] a few times; they are still alright.[17]

These boys had just been through the first major offensive action for the 32nd. They were part of the Aisne-Marne Campaign, also known as the Second Battle of the Marne, in the region of Château Thierry. The 127th Infantry went over the top on July 30, 1918. Some eight days later, the division had captured the railhead and stronghold of Fismes and had pushed the Germans back across the Vesle River. It was here that the division earned the nickname of "*Les Terribles*" from the French officer who observed the battle.[18]

WITH ARNOLD HANSEN AND THE
121ST MACHINE GUN BATTALION

Arnold Hansen trained at Camp MacArthur with the other Brooklyn boys and crossed the pond at the same time, but he was in Company D, 121st Machine Gun Battalion, and thus also remained with the 32nd Division. He wrote to his parents on August 9:

Have not had much time to write lately, as we have been on the move for the last few days, and it has been what I call an exciting time. To begin with, they pulled us out of the sector we were in when I last wrote, and then began a three-day hike. Next move we were loaded on the train "to somewhere in France." Our little joy ride lasted two days, then more hiking until we came to a big woods. Here we camped for two days, then we were taken in trucks, which brought us to a place where we found real war going on. We have been going at the Germans to beat the band for a few days and are now

expecting a rest, whether we get it or not; they change the
orders in the army so many times that it keeps a fellow guess-
ing as to what is next.

I saw Einar Johnson last night; he is getting along fine.
Our company is attached to the same battalion that he is in.
Have not heard from the rest of the Brooklyn boys [those
who went with the First Division]. Must close as there is not
much to write.[19]

About a month later, in sequential issues in mid- to late October, two more letters from Hansen appeared in the *Brooklyn
Teller*, describing what he was able to of the progress of the 32nd.
The first was addressed to his parents and was likely written in
early September.

Just had a chance to take part in another big drive on the
Germans. You no doubt will read in the paper on what front
it was. Our division once more lived up to its old standard by
gaining its objective. Our company was exceptionally lucky as
we had very few casualties.

We are now back of the line and will have one more hitch
on the front; then we go back for a rest, and it sure will be a
treat because a fellow has his hands full ducking the German
shells, and fighting the cooties [lice]. As yet we have no way
of getting rid of them. Will close as there is no news we can
write.[20]

The second letter, dated September 12 was addressed to
his uncle:

Just a few lines to let you know that I am well and alive, although we have seen some pretty lively scraps lately. You no
doubt have read in the papers what has been going on. Well,

we were finally relieved and sent back for a few days' rest, and then hiked up to a different front. On the way up we had a chance to see what damage artillery can do. We passed village after village that had been blown up by big shells.

The morning we went on the front line was sure a pretty sight. Our artillery opened on the German lines just at day break, we could see the shells bursting on the German lines and the flare from the rockets made a red light across the whole front and then the fun began. We were busy during the day ducking machine gun bullets and big shells. They have anything but a musical sound. Our progress for the first few days was rather slow on account of so many German machine gun nests. After they were cleaned out, we had clear sailing. But the Germans sure put up a fight where they got a chance, especially where they know that the Americans are fighting them. The Wisconsin boys sure have kept up the old Wisconsin war standard.

Crops over here are looking fine and at many places the German prisoners are harvesting the grain. They sure have a bunch of prisoners, and most of them seem to be glad to be taken prisoners. The infantry boys have found a number of Germans chained to machine guns, and made to shoot to the last. So from that, imagine they are tired of war and are forced to continue against their own will.

Well, must close,

Arnold Hansen[21]

WITH REQUARTTE HAHN AND THE SUPPLY COMPANY OF THE 121st FIELD ARTILLERY

Requartte Hahn of the Brodhead area was with the supply company of the 121st Field Artillery, which supported the 32nd

Division. He trained with the 127th and 128th Infantries at
Waco, but his job with the supply company, although certainly
not without danger, was not as grim as being a machine-gunner or
infantryman. Two letters from Hahn written in the late summer
of 1918 were published in Brodhead newspapers. The first was
dated August 21.

Dear Folks,

It is nearly dark and I must hurry that my letters may not
be too short. I am sitting in front of a dugout using an old box
and a German shell basket as a table and chair.

It is going to be another good moonlight night and Fritz is
pretty sure to be around. Of course, he has only a few planes
and may not send them here. Anyway, it looks that way to us.
Another thing, of all the shells and bombs he drops around,
the most of them are "duds" (do not explode). It is fun to hear
the fellows in the dugout, nights when the shells start coming—ZZZZZZ plunk; Oh, H___ another dud.

It's a funny thing about this place where we are now;
shells drop all around, but never seem to find us. It is so dark I
can hardly see the paper. Will finish tomorrow.[22]

The letter that followed was dated September 1.

Dear Folks:

Received four letters from you today. It had been over two
weeks since hearing from you, but we have been on the move
all the time and one could hardly expect mail.

What do you think of the 32nd division now? To say the
least they have been doing some wonderful work, and the fellows have been worked pretty hard, but a couple good nights'
sleep makes everything fine again.

Men of the 127th Infantry, 32nd Division gather at a dugout
entrance on the Alsatian front. WHI IMAGE ID 111689

I probably could tell you a lot of things you would like to
know that have ceased to be interesting to us. When one is at
the front he crawls in his hole and stays there, that is when a
German barrage is put over. Then you have a little excitement
once in a while when German prisoners are brought in, some
of them fourteen to sixteen years old. The fellows found a
couple of kids (Germans) in a dugout the other day and they
were bawling to beat the band. Of course there are others besides kids over the top of this hill out here.

I will be glad when a fellow can get a real sleep again. You just about get to sleep when there comes a gas alarm. One fumbles around and gets his gas mask on and lies down again; then the all clear is given and you try to go to sleep again. About that time an old "well digger" comes over, then a couple of duds (dead ones), then another live one; and all of a sudden a Boche drops six big pills around you. Then machine guns start booming, rockets go up and huge search lights are played on the sky. Such is a night, and still a fellow goes to bed and never thinks anything about it. Dad, those well diggers make a hole big enough to put our barn in.

[Continued the next day] I got up about seven this morning, had flap jacks for breakfast. I had a pretty good night's sleep, even if they were shelling pretty heavy. I ate breakfast with Kenneth Olson, that's all of the fellows from home I have seen in the last few days, but by asking the other fellows, I find they are all well. Well I must close now.

With love,

Requartte

THE QUESTION OF
GERMAN AMERICAN LOYALTY

The Wisconsin boys had reason to be sensitive about their contribution to the war effort, as much had been made of Wisconsin's supposed disloyalty. Those overseas tried to prove their patriotism on the battlefield, while those at home did so by buying Liberty Bonds and supporting the Red Cross. The towns in Green County had been sparring in Liberty Bond competition.

At the end of October 1917, the *Monticello Messenger* had printed all the names of those who had bought bonds for the second Liberty Loan Drive and all the names of the 210 members of the local Red Cross unit. "Is your name on the list?" the newspaper article asked. "If it isn't, see to it that it gets there at once."[23] Just the week before, an article in the *Monticello Messenger* with the headline "Monroe Paper Takes Hard Slam at Monticello" quoted the *Monroe Evening Times* accusing Monticello of failing to cooperate with the Liberty Loan Drive.[24] Each county and each community within the county were given quotas; thus every family had a responsibility to buy bonds.[25]

When Charles Marshall wrote home in May 1918, he commented on the news of the third Liberty Loan Drive. "I was glad to hear that you were successful in the Liberty Loan Drive. I noticed Wisconsin was one of the first states to come through in the big drive. Old Wisconsin has a lot of men in service, who will show what old Wisconsin can do."[26]

Requartte Hahn, who had German grandparents, was also glad to hear the news of the successful drive, and he commented on how he felt to be an American:

> There is no place like the U.S.A. and the people like you that have made it the greatest and most powerful nation in the world. You home there in Wisconsin don't realize what it is, but if you could be in a foreign country and get up and say, "I'm from the U.S.A." you would see what it means. I'm proud to be her servant and proud of those who have made her what she is. For instance the Third Liberty Loan comes along and you raise the amount in four hours. You know that makes the old Kaiser's head swim.[27]

Edwin Barlow wrote two letters to the editor of the *Monticello Messenger* in the late summer of 1918 in which he commented on his own German heritage and his growing bitterness toward the Germans. Edwin worked in the same hospital unit with his cousin Reuel, but he worked much more closely with the wounded men.

While it is pleasant to care for the sick and wounded, it is rather nerve racking to be compelled to stand by and fight with the Grim Reaper, knowing the odds are against you and that you are helpless to save them. On several occasions it has happened that I have found myself alone with the patients as they crossed the divide. All were brave. All were happy and rejoiced in the fact that they were giving their young lives for their country, with always a thought of the loved ones back home. Often in the night, you would hear someone call for mother; I find that mother is the last word a dying man usually forms.

Truly, at times like these I feel like grabbing a gun and becoming a real soldier. I feel I have a strength and hatred enough in my carcass to lick a whole German regiment single-handed. They have bombed another hospital—these barbarians. To be bombed when one is fit and active is part of the game. But to lie here unable to move with fever making you a bit light-headed, pain giving you a dread of any further shock or blow, to hear those awful explosions going on nearby, to feel that any moment it may be your turn to go through it— that is something I don't believe hell could beat.

When I see and hear of the atrocities of the Huns, do you know that I detest and loathe the fact that I can speak their damnable language. If there are any pro-Germans in Monticello, I wish they could get a dose of Boche "kultur" in the shape of shrapnel, followed by a gargle of German. When I was in the States, I had always given Germany the benefit of the doubt as to the crimes she was credited with committing. Seeing is believing, however; therefore my bitterness.[28]

Some three weeks later he wrote again discussing German war atrocities and his bitter feelings.

Green County was among the districts in Wisconsin said to be "most infected with Pro-Germanism." Merely supporting Senator Bob LaFollette or James Thompson, who contended for the Republican nomination in a 1918 Senate primary, was enough to be branded 'disloyal' by the Wisconsin Loyalty League. WHI IMAGE ID 40882

I have seen things with my own eyes and felt things that I have read and heard about, but never believed until now. Every moment I am here, I experience a growing anger at the Germans. I cannot find a word that will properly express the anger and bitter contempt I have for these barbarians. When one assists at an operating table twenty out of twenty-four hours, sees and hears the stories of the atrocities they commit upon our own boys, it makes one feel like cutting the throat of every pro-German to avenge the death of those brave lads.

A hospital corps man was found dead in an open field, having
been deliberately shot by a sniper while on duty in broad day
light. The Red Cross brassard showed plainly upon his arm
but did not save him.

Anyone with pro-German ideas, I don't care who they
are, should be compelled to come over here and get a taste of
"kultur" the Kaiser defends and represents. It's all very well
and good to talk and air your views 4,000 miles from the battlefields. Just let them walk about this battle front; then let me
take them through the hospital. I am sure they would change
their views.[29]

Edwin Barlow had no doubt read about German sympathizers
in the *Monticello Messenger*.

Monticello had many German speakers among its citizens,
and the German Reformed Church was well attended. In March
1918, the German Reformed Church had hosted a patriotic
meeting with a speaker of German heritage from the University
of Wisconsin. He was "sent here under the auspices of the county
council of defense."[30] On July 10, 1918, the *Messenger* reported
that the Justice Department had been paying visits to pro-Germans in the area, including four men in Brodhead and two in
Juda. The article stated that "some heretofore active pro-Germans promised to be good, in fact very good, in the future. One
man was found with a revolver and some fifty cartridges in his
possession which he gave up with emphatic promises not to talk
any more German and to take his share and more in all war activities in the future." The article stated that this individual was
known in the vicinity as "Kaiser Bill." Another man was visited
because he "was recently in an encounter with a Brodhead dray-
man for talking German." Both men reportedly promised their
future American loyalty.[31]

WITH MAJOR LORENZ AS THE 32ND
MOVED TOWARD JUVIGNY

Many of the letters printed in the Green County newspapers from the boys who fought in World War I were filled with rather mundane details: how many letters they just received, what they ate for breakfast, whether the package from Aunt Harriet arrived, or how wonderful it was to receive the *Monticello Messenger* or the *Brodhead News*. In part because their letters were censored, and in part because they didn't know what to say about the war—right there in the midst of it—most letters contained only glimpses of the war and the work of the men who fought the battles.

The following letter from Major Lorenz is exceptional. Written to his wife during the first week of September 1918 and printed in the *Brodhead News* in mid-October, the letter describes in surprising detail the movement of the 32nd Division toward the battle at the village of Juvigny just north of Soissons, and the work of the field hospital during that major battle. Major Lorenz was in the same field hospital unit with Reuel Barlow of Monticello and Elmer Swann of Brodhead.

Lorenz wrote home on September 4.

Quite suddenly one night, while we were resting at Reddy farm (this is the area through which our division made its great advance north of Château Thierry, now generally spoken of as the "Ourcq to the Veale"), I received an order to pack at once and move with the "train" at zero hour. Much would be later communicated. We hustled and loaded our trucks, the men getting on and sleeping on top of the load. About midnight the order to move came, and I led my eight trucks with two side cars, carrying Lieutenant Draper and

Lieutenant Thompson, out on the road and took my place in
a long line of moving trucks. All was done at night time with
as little noise as possible and absolutely no light.

Yet the noise attracted some Boche planes that are always
soaring around overhead, and a few bombs were dropped
in our vicinity. Fortunately, no one was hurt. Then the train
moved on along the road. Our ultimate destination we did
not know. We had maps furnished us and had to guide our
own course within certain limitations. At daybreak we pulled
off the road into a big forest and everyone threw himself
down anywhere and slept. Meanwhile a fire was started and
coffee and bacon with hardtack was served.

Later in the morning we pulled out again and rolled
along for the rest of the day, stopping toward evening for a
brief rest. Knowing our general direction, we began to plan
at what point in the line our division would be stopped.
These movements were made at least 20 miles in back of the
battlefield. Soon our ultimate destination loomed up. It was
to be at the Aisne, north of Soissons. Toward evening we
pulled into a big forest of beechnuts, tremendous trees with
foliage only at the top. We rolled into this forest and were
directed to a certain place to camp, no one knew how long.
Soon the men had the pup tents set up, a guard was posted
and supper prepared. Other parts of our division came up
and went into the forest. Soon we were surrounded by everything—infantry, artillery, and the whole division, hidden
away in the woods.

The men all began to prepare bomb proofs, and my officers and I built one for ourselves. By using empty ammunition boxes filled with sand, we made quite an enclosure
which was covered by canvas. The walls of our shelter were
about four feet high, sufficient to protect us from flying shrapnel when we lay on our cots. Of course, a direct hit means

extermination, but there are few such and after a while one really becomes a little indifferent to the whole affair, a fatalist.

That night, when all was settled and darkness was coming on, my men camped about 50 yards from me, began singing. I can't describe the sensation; it was the most impressive thing I ever experienced in all my life. Here was an entire division of over 20,000 troops, camped on the floor of a big forest. In the gloom one could see horses, mules, trucks, machine guns, artillery and what-not gathered in orderly groups, soldiers everywhere, first in subdued silence. Then groups of men starting singing together—plaintive, then rollicking, and finally "On Wisconsin." I believe it thrilled everybody within hearing. I walked up and found that already several hundred men were gathered in a circle listening. Within a few more days many of those standing around would be no more, except in memory. Those thoughts kept coming to my mind because I suspected a big battle was about to be fought. I was not depressed, but the solemnity of it all impressed me very much. Soon it was quite dark, and then a great silence fell. The occasional whinnering of a horse, or restlessness of a mule was all that could be heard, and everybody slept.

In the great darkness one could hear the sentries going on their posts and all was quiet, when suddenly a tremendous explosion, then another and another, with smaller ones interspersed, and at the same time the hum of the motor of a German *avion* would be heard almost overhead. One knew at once what had happened; the enemy planes had started high in the heavens, shut off their motors and sailed down quietly and quickly as a bird, soaring easily, unheard and unsuspected. As soon as their bombs were dropped, they started their motors again.

Our anti-aircraft guns opened up, and the din was terrible for a half hour or so. The planes kept dropping big and little

A German plane brought down near Montfaucon, France. WHI IMAGE ID
132646

bombs around, until unloaded; one dropped a big flare bomb
that lighted up the surroundings for several minutes. With
this light to guide him, the aviator opened up with his machine gun on some troops that were still on the road and bullets whistled through the leaves of the trees nearby. This was a
typical attack by airplane on troops bivouacked in woods.

Soon the anti-aircraft guns made it too hot for them and
they pulled away. The hum of their motors became dim, and
soon everything was quiet again. From experience we knew
we were likely to be left alone until about 4:00 a.m. This
morning we were more fortunate for no further visits took
place. We remained nestled in the woods all day.

That night, about midnight, I received an order by courier
to send an officer to a certain place and get maps and orders.
I sent Lieutenant Draper in a side car. All traveling you know
is done without lights, on roads loaded with all sorts of traffic,
so that it is no easy task to take such a trip. He returned and
I opened my order, which was secret. At 4:00 a.m. I was to

leave the woods and join others at a certain cross road. I had my company awakened at 2:30 a.m. and at 4:00 we stole out on the road, got to our place and shortly after started on our way nearer the battle front. By noon we reached the Aisne. Here again were the same kind of pontoon bridges we had crossed down on the Marne. My orders were to remain in the vicinity of a certain town, or rather what is left of that town. We pulled our trucks off the road under trees and camouflaged as well as we could. Now we could easily hear the battle ahead of us, big guns were in action and not infrequently a particularly big German gun would drop a shell not far away. They were trying for the bridges.

We remained there all day, though I received orders to go up and pick out a place for an Advanced Surgical Hospital and "Triage." I found an old château badly shot away, yet some rooms could be fixed up for operating rooms. The roads in and out were good for ambulances so I decided on this

The ruins of a church in Neuville, France, served as a field hospital for wounded American soldiers. WHI IMAGE ID 132653

place. Had to persuade some French who were there that I had authority from the highest course, that the place was at my disposal. One must frequently do a little of this bluffing business to get what one wants. I also selected a place for a "Triage," the function of which I will explain some time.

As night came on, our infantry began passing us on the road, fellows we know would be greeted, and a "Good Luck" would be passed, also "Give 'em Hell," "Remember the 32nd," "You know what you did to them at Château Thierry." Then artillery rumbled by and soon we moved into our new and final position for the battle. All these movements are made at night, when everything is inky black. You can't imagine the difficulties. Men must walk in front of trucks so they can keep on the road. Then the shell holes! If one falls into one of these in the dark a broken neck might be the souvenir, while a truck or automobile will be almost ruined and certainly put out of commission.

After a while we reached our new home, the old château and trucks were unloaded, tentage put up, rooms cleaned out, wooden horses put up to put litters on. Operations are done right on litters, you know, the same one the soldier is placed on when picked up on the field. One never changes a man from one litter to another. The tentage for the Triage was set up nearer the main road, and I sent word by courier to headquarters that Field Hospital 127 was ready, where it and the Triage were. Then we sat down and waited and listened to the battle in front of us.

I knew of course, that our first brigade was to go in at a certain time, and knew from experience when I could expect the wounded to arrive.

Our objective was Juvigny. It had held out a long while and formed the peak of a wedge in the line, the point sticking out toward us. Our division was to take that town at all costs.

You know we were the only American division in the battle
and had been called up here by the French for this particular
task. Our division was specifically mentioned to do the job.
We were not and are not, this minute associated with any
American corps, but form a part of the French 10th army
corps under General Mangin.

Our first brigade went in at the time fixed and drove
ahead. The rest of that night a terrible battle raged ahead of
us. Soon the wounded began arriving and all of us began to
work. Everybody was occupied; all in darkness everywhere
except in two rooms fixed up as operating rooms, and here
the windows or rather the window frames (because all the
glass is shot away), were covered with blankets. Soon four
wounded are brought in on litters and given ether. Two officers at each litter compose the operating team. Only the
worst cases are taken in here, so you can hardly picture the
frightful sights that soon become commonplace. The work
went on all night. Occasionally a bomb or a shell dropped
nearby, yet no one stopped. Once in a while when one of
these came a little close, all you heard was a muttered curse by
somebody. The Americans are certainly a profane bunch, but
somehow the profanity is not really thought of in that light. It
is merely an outlet for suppressed feelings.

The next day our other brigade went in, and soon we
heard from the wounded about the progress made. It was a
terrific fight here. The Germans resisted with machine guns
and artillery, but they could not stop our boys! Finally one
night they got to the outskirts of the town and by the following morning had driven the enemy out and almost six miles
beyond. In fact they drove them so far that the flanks or sides
were exposed, the French not having made equal progress on
either side, so that our division had to wait a whole day until
this distance was made up on the sides. Meantime the steady

stream of wounded increased and five days and nights we worked incessantly.

I worked mainly at the Triage. This is a sorting station to which all wounded come and are separated into those who can be passed onto the rear in ambulances, and those who, owing to their serious condition, must be operated on at once. Owing to the lack of officers and rush of work, I did this all alone, night and day, simply snatching a little sleep whenever a lull permitted. I did not have my clothes off in over seven days, not even my cap or Sam Browne belt.[32] We work in advance of the advance surgical hospital, which was also mine. I had with me 30 men as litter bearers, etc. It is an important piece of work and difficult under the conditions. We must work at night, and if we show the slightest light, we are rewarded with a few bombs.

The night activity in the air is an awesome sight. In the midst of our work, we will hear the hum of several German planes, then the nearby anti-aircraft guns open up and then most wonderful of all, powerful search lights throw beams of light into the heavens, moving about constantly trying to pick up a plane. Occasionally they do and we have seen such brought down by the anti-aircraft guns. Yet in spite of all this noise and hell going on all around us, our work goes on without confusion or halt. Of course every once in a while I am forced to take a situation in hand by rather forcible language, but generally everything goes well, and our work becomes better and better.

During this battle we handled a large number of German prisoners. Our men brought in a great many: some were very young and all seemed glad to be taken prisoners, except the officers. We care for the severely wounded at our place, just as we do our own, only they must wait until our own are taken

care of. We give them hot coffee and bread, for which they are
very thankful.

Now the battle is over, and our division has again covered
itself with glory. Our commanding general said his division
was the best in the whole U.S.A. army. We all think so. We
have passed through our second big battle in about six weeks.
Soon there will be many new faces in our ranks, but the spirit
will continue.

We are now known as the "Shock Division" and where we
go to next will be a place where they need a real fighting unit.
I have not been able to relate one-tenth part of what I saw
during this battle. A thousand things come to my mind this
minute, but I can't write them all. I hope time will not wipe
it out, because my experiences must be of interest to you and
the boys.

From your husband, camped near the banks of the Aisne,
near Soissons.[33]

Part of the letter above was saved for the following issue of
the *Brodhead News* and was then published with this additional
letter dated September 7:

We have been taken out of the line completely and are now
resting in the same big beech wood forest I mentioned in my
last letter. As I wrote, the part played by our division sand-
wiched in between the French north of Soissons was a huge
success and our regimental flags have been sent for in order
that these standards may receive decoration; the first received
by any American Division over here or during this war. The
French call this division the "Division Terrible," and the "ace"
of the American divisions. It is said that the Germans want to
sign a separate peace with the 32nd.

From prisoners we get some interesting tales, for instance, early in the fight they saw the drab uniform—there having been no Americans up here, they thought we were English, until during a charge, instead of our soldiers stopping when several nests of machine guns opened up on them, they kept on coming. They knew then that these must be Americans and possibly the same they had heard of at Château Thierry; true enough. The number of prisoners taken by our troops was very large in spite of what they are told by their officers. I got this myself from a wounded German; that his officers told him by no means to be taken prisoner because the Americans always cut the throats of their prisoners. The poor devil believed this and was wondering all the time when it was to happen. He was shot in the arm as he tried to escape from a shell hole in front and was then brought in by one of our boys. There are a great number of young men, almost boys, among those taken. All say they are 19 years old but many appear to be 17. As I mentioned, we treat these poor fellows very well indeed, the wounded receive the same care that our own do and they are very thankful and surprised.

I have not the slightest idea where we go from here, possibly they may give us a real rest. On the other hand, there may be a real job to do somewhere and we will be sent to do it. By the way, with this second citation of our division, we, that is all of the division who were with it through the period, can wear from their left shoulder a braided cord. Some call it a "curtain cord." It is green with tassels, you may have seen it in pictures. I don't know whether the Americans will be allowed this distinctive mark. It is conferred by the French. With a few more fights to our credit, we will be decked out like peacocks.[34]

Shortly after Major Lorenz wrote that last letter to his wife, the 32nd did move to a rest area briefly, from September 10 to 22. During that time, the division received about five thousand replacements and engaged in a training program. General Pershing came to congratulate the men of the 32nd on their fine work and to help to inspire them for their next go around.[35] They would indeed have more battles to fight.

REUEL BARLOW WRITES OF
LIFE AT THE FRONT

The 32nd Division moved back to the front line as part of the First American Army in the Meuse-Argonne offensive. In this third and final major offensive, the 32nd became the first Allied division to pierce the German Hindenburg Line of defense. It then proceeded to capture the final German stronghold at Kriemhilde Stellung, after fighting continuously for twenty days from the end of September to October 19, in cold and rainy conditions. Following this operation, the 32nd became known as the Red Arrow Division, and it adopted the insignia, for its shoulder patch, of a line shot through with a red arrow.

Reuel Barlow began writing another letter to the editor of the *Monticello Messenger* just as the 32nd Division was getting ready to move into action. In a letter dated September 26, he wrote of life at the front; of Fred Amstutz, the young sergeant from Monticello who was killed in action; and of the sounds at night over the battlefield:

Since May, I have been at the front, with the exception of
a week's rest recently out of the zone of advance, and the
short periods in which we were traveling via truck from one
part of the line to another. Even then we got under shell fire

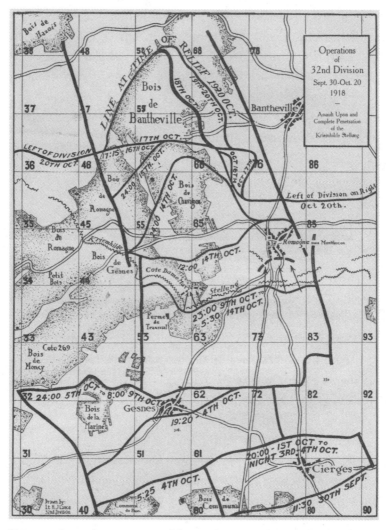

This map shows the movement of the 32nd Division from September 30 to October 20, 1918. During this time, the division penetrated the German stronghold of the Kriemhilde Stellung to earn the title of Red Arrow Division. *THE 32ND DIVISION IN THE WORLD WAR, 1917–1919*, P. 96

on several occasions. But generally our rides were through the quiet rural districts, down shady winding roads and out on large crowded main highways. The roads of France are wonderful and certainly ought to make motoring a pleasure in peace times. We travel night and day, without lights at night. Even cigarettes are banned at night. The Boche aviator goes for a show of fire like these mammoth French bees do for flies. Many times I have heard the warning, "Put that light out or I'll shoot it out." There is nothing that will cause you to jump on your best friend so quick, as for him to light a cigarette in the battle area.

Just now the big guns are knocking the top off a long ridge over here, and I feel sorry for the Germans when the Americans and French let loose. The Americans fire the French gun six times as fast as the French do, because they load it on the recoil. I have heard German prisoners myself ask what kind of "machine-gun artillery" the Americans have, because they shoot so rapidly. The French are afraid the gun will jam and blow up. Not so the Americans. They pack her full and let her go.

I talked with Fred Amstutz the night when we moved up the Château Thierry front. We were both stopped along the road on the banks of the Marne and I ran down the road a ways when I saw his company stop. Both he and Sam were in fine spirits, and the record made by them is more thrilling and more heroic than anything that we have ever read in American history. As a result of that record, our division was picked by the French to storm a point on another part of the line which the French had attacked time and again. And you haven't read of anything that looked like failure in what the Americans have attempted, have you?

I am glad to read of so many of the home boys being over here. Now I have gotten so that I keep on the look-out and maybe sometime I'll run across some of them. They will soon be fighting cooties and feel the rats brushing against their ears. A fellow gets so that he soon learns quite a little about

American soldiers are being deloused after returning from the front lines.
Montfaucon, Meuse, France, October 22, 1918. WHI IMAGE ID 132716

the habits of cooties, for they are a very intelligent beast. Of
course a fellow doesn't continue peaceful relations with them
more than a day when he is in a place where he can get water
and has a change of underclothing. One of the soldier's greatest victories is when he learns to sleep soundly after suddenly
discovering that a battalion of cooties has advanced upon
him. The tricks they play after they have gained their object
are really laughable. They can maneuver in single file around
your waist, or do guard duty back and forth on your spinal
column with the ease of a hard-boiled "Reg." Needless to say,
no human being will consent to being a drill field for more
than ten hours, and the Medical Department has the means
of putting the kibosh on little cootie in short order.[36]

Barlow put his letter aside and picked it up again October 6.
He continued:

We have been up and doing since I wrote you the above. We have been under shell fire four days. The Heinies send them over day and night, and I have gotten now so that I can rise up at night at the first whistle of a shell coming over and do the "shell flop" into a dugout before the thing goes off. I have got it timed so harmoniously that I generally hit the floor of the dugout just as the bang sounds from above.

But the Boche have been pushed back now so that today has been quiet. I sleep in the edge of a woods with my bunk "behind" a tree three feet in diameter and no roof over my head. At night I can see only the trunks of the shell-stripped trees against the sky. And the sounds I can hear are certainly interesting. Our own artillery is behind us and it bangs and snuffs out our candles and shakes things up in general. Also I can hear, besides our own big guns, the sound of machine gun fire off to the northeast, and then the whistle and bang of shells coming over. Usually a couple Boche planes buzz around after dark overhead, and the anti-aircraft guns boom away. Down the valley are thousands of moving vehicles, trucks, ambulances, and artillery pieces. Added to this last night were several score tanks, sounding like threshing machines crawling along. A spectacular sight at night is to see the sheets of flame that burst from the big guns, situated in a straight line along a ridge as far as one can see. And when they open up it makes one feel mighty good, for we know the Hun is getting his.

We have been working pretty furious. My work is making records and reports on casualties and there is nothing about it that resembles office work back in civilian life.

I wish I could describe the immense forces lying back in the valleys around here and the scenes I have witnessed in a certain little valley where once there were many villages, but now nothing is discernable but the foundations of buildings and a few crumbled walls, around which swarm thousands of Americans, with all their paraphernalia. We see German planes fall every day and air battles every few hours.

The other day a German came over and shot down an observation balloon. The balloon was almost hauled down when the German swooped at it in a last attempt and succeeded in setting it afire. But he was hit himself, landed in a nook in the valley where the ground was covered with American troops. His plane turned end over end, but the German was able to run and he started off for the woods. A couple Americans took after him and caught him in a jiffy.

There are many such little incidents to tell, but it would make this letter too long. It is time I was in bed anyway.

I am fine and hope this finds you in the best of health. Tell them all "hello" at home. Hope to see you all a year from now—if not sooner.

Sincerely, from the other side of the Hindenburg line.

Reuel R. Barlow[37]

WITH THE 32ND IN THE FINAL MONTH OF BATTLE

In the midst of that same Meuse-Argonne offensive, on October 12, Requartte Hahn wrote to his parents.

Dear Folks,

When you were [last] writing you had just received the letters I had written while on the Marne drive. I will have a whole lot to tell you of that when I get home. It will surely go down in history. After we got done there, we fought on the Soissons front; that was as bad. Now we are at another front, in my opinion the worst of all. We did not get the long rest we expected and came right back into line again. It has gotten to be a regular life now; a fellow can be in bed and listen to the old well diggers come over and think nothing of it. Z-Z-Z-Z-Z-Z-Boom—and the dirt flies.

I see the other fellows from home quite often and they are all getting along fine—that is the fellows in this regiment. The others I haven't seen for some time. I am always planning on running across Wilbert [Murphy], but somehow I never get a chance to see him; and I would like to see Charles Marshall.

You have probably read of how an enemy plane flies low along a road and uses a machine gun down the column Well I happened to be in one of those incidents the other day, but the guy didn't get very far before the plane fell to the ground about a block ahead of where I was.

Well I must close now. Will write just as often as possible. My love to grandmother.[38]

Before the armistice, Reuel Barlow wrote two more letters to his parents that were published in the *Monticello Messenger*.[39] In a letter dated October 23, he wrote:

Just a line to let you know we are back for a rest, which promises to be a long one, and that some of our fellows have gone on their furloughs. I haven't put my name in yet, but will do so when the next bunch is permitted to leave. Expect to be around here a couple of months.

We have seen some exciting events. During our last three weeks at the front, I have had mud and rocks splashed around me by shells, and two fellows were killed outright not very far away. Also the aeroplanes at night came pretty close with

their bombs, but we always got into dugouts where nothing
could reach us.

We have not received a *Messenger* in several weeks. Please
send clippings of any letters from soldiers in the *Messenger*,
also anything else of interest.

I am in the best of health and spirits. We are not in a civi-
lized country yet, but hope to be so situated in another week
or two. No stores and not even a building standing here, but it
isn't like the place we just left, for that was a very recent battle
field covered with all kinds of wreckage. This place is cleaned
up and not over-run with troops, anyway.

We are all going to get entire new clothing, equipment,
etc. You should have seen us, even yesterday. Mud plastered
over everything—everything bedraggled and dirty, hair long,
and almost everyone with whiskers all over their faces. We
can still see the flare and hear the rumble of artillery and see
German aeroplanes, but it is not like when you are in action
at the front.

Do you read the Madison papers? They have been printing a lot about us and the Madison boys whom we are with.
We were in Château Thierry and at Juvigny, near Soissons,
and of course you know we were in Alsace. We had some recent action that had any of the others beat, but it is so recent I
cannot mention anything about it.

Barlow's letter of November 3 reads in part,

We are still in the land of devastation, but not in action. There
is nothing taking place here, so I can write very little. I sent
you the last issue of the *Stars and Stripes*. I do not think it will
be giving away any military information if I say I have gone
over that road.

There isn't much to write about except the village here, which is almost as completely gone as it could be. It must have been destroyed in 1914, for only a few stones show where a wall was and the grass has grown over everything.

Am sending you a piece of shrapnel. This is a small piece; some pieces are as long as your hand. I have seen pieces like this taken out of a fellow's intestines. It's bad stuff. This was picked up in some old German trenches, probably fired by Americans. The ground is covered with it here and every post and tree is filled with steel and lead.

During these last few weeks of war, Elmer Dixon wrote a letter with a rather unique perspective. Dixon enlisted with the National Guard and trained in Waco with the 32nd Division; when he crossed the Atlantic, he landed at Liverpool and spent time at a hospital there. Separated from his regiment, he took an opportunity to join the 301st Heavy Tank Battalion and spent several weeks in training. In the final months of the war, the 301st supported various divisions at the front.[40] Dixon was officially "at rest" when he wrote to his sister on October 31.

Dear Sister:

I know you will think I have forgotten home altogether for the last six weeks, but it just couldn't be helped—or is it eight weeks? I hardly had time to think of home, or time for anything.

We were in four shows and now we are back a ways for a rest. I don't suppose I dare tell you how badly we were damaged, but I'd rather not anyway because it's not the most pleasant thing in the world to write or talk about. Most of us have been quite busy the last few days cleaning up—getting rid of cooties mostly—and getting respectable looking

Two companies of tanks assisted the 32nd Division, seen here near Juvigny,
France. WHI IMAGE ID 131015

clothing on again. It's a great life, but it wasn't so bad after the
first show, probably because Fritz found it a little too warm
for him and decided to travel. We fared pretty well the last
two shows because we went so far as to rob his gardens and
fields of vegetables and grain. We found fresh vegetables of all
kinds and much prettier country because everything wasn't
shot up so bad. Even the villages look half-way respectable.
We also released thousands of civilians, so you see we are not
going to feel downhearted even though we have cause for it.
I don't know what they intend to do with us now. Of course I
couldn't tell you if I did, but we can at least breathe freely for
a while anyway.

I'm really not off duty, even though we are back for a rest,
for I belong to Headquarter Co. A few others and I are supposed to be mechanics and able to bring in tanks when they
go wrong or knocked out, or probably of more importance,
able to fix all little minor troubles that sometimes occur just

before we send them over the top, in other words—give
them a start. It's really a repair unit and we generally try to
bring in the tanks that are not too badly damaged or ditched
shortly after a show. But you see we have many out there
that require two and three days' work on, especially if one
has been bombed up. So Headquarter work isn't really over
until the best of them are in. It's generally a case of rob one
to complete another and then tow it in with the other. We
have a big truck with us all the time with repairs of all kinds.
By the way—we lost our truck driver in the second show so I
am driving it every time we go out. We are off in the morning
for about a two-day siege with orders to bring in a tank that
had been burned. I'm trying to write this letter by the light of
a candle on the edge of my bed. The bed consists of a ground
sheet and two blankets on Mother Earth—and the d——
candle refuses to stand up for me.

> Your loving brother,
> Sergeant E.L. Dixon[41]

ON THE MOVE WITH THE FIRST DIVISION

By November 11 when armistice was declared, the 32nd Division
had worked very hard and had made quite a name for itself. But
those Wisconsin boys who were transferred to the First Division
spent even more time on active fronts. The First Division arrived
first in France, and Pershing relied on it for the vital sectors.
The First made a total advance against German resistance of
fifty-one kilometers. By comparison, the 32nd Division advanced
thirty-six kilometers.[42]

The First Division entered the Picardy region of northern
France on April 25 and won the first American victory of the
war with the capture of the village of Cantigny with an operation

that began on May 28. The division then held the village against repeated German counterattacks and continued the advance until it was finally relieved July 7. On July 17 the First Division went back to the line for the Soissons operation, and also participated in the major battles of St. Mihiel and the Meuse-Argonne offensive.

Some of the boys transferred from the 32nd to the First Division were promptly wounded or killed. Sam Schmid of Monticello, for example, was killed on May 30 in the action at Cantigny.[43]

Wilbert Murphy was transferred into Company D of the 28th Infantry in the First Division, and his early letters clearly reflected that getting used to life in the trenches was not easy for him. But he kept at it. While he was at the front, his letters contained few descriptions of his activities there, but the letters show how the hard service changed his thinking and attitude.

On June 17 he wrote,

> Just recently, Mother, I came out of the trenches from another tour in them. I surely will be glad if I am always lucky as I have been. One surely can have some narrow escapes from the big shells that sing overhead and occasionally drop uncomfortably close to your hole in the ground—for the trenches are nothing more than ditches with occasionally a shelter overhead for protection from the shrapnel. These high explosive shells of Fritz's surely have me buffaloed, and I like to keep down when the shells are coming.
>
> I [last] wrote to you from the hospital where I was sent for a few days, but am well now and feeling fine. I just had a fever that I got in the trenches and I got over it easily.
>
> The weather was fine all the time in the trenches and is continuing so. I shouldn't have told you I was in the trenches because now I am afraid you will be worrying. But don't

worry, just think that God will take care of us and what he causes to happen will take place.

We are billeted now in a good-looking French town and are getting a much needed rest. It seems good to get away from the sound of the guns. It gets on my nerves. Bombardments and barrages are nerve racking worlds of noise, clouds of smoke, and showers of rock and shrapnel. There is a Y.M.C.A. where we can buy cookies and sweets and get paper to write on, and then there is a Red Cross here. They give away hot chocolate and "smokes" and treat us fine.

With lots of love, Wilbert[44]

About six weeks later, on July 28, Murphy wrote to his folks:

Well here it is Sunday again and things are going about as usual. I am feeling fine and enjoying life.

You want to know how often I had been in the trenches. Well I can't say exactly, but I am free to say, I guess, that I have been at several different fronts, more than six times altogether; and talk about experience! Shell fire is the worst thing to contend with because it is so hard on the nerves. But it doesn't worry us. Shell fire or no shell fire, we do our duty and succeed. I have been in attacks too, and gone "over the top" a number of times. Going over isn't so bad after the first time—that is, it don't worry one a great deal after the first time. There isn't anything to worry about anyway, because if one is going to get bumped off, he will, and "going over" won't make any difference.[45]

Nearly two months later, on September 25, Murphy wrote,

We have moved again and are waiting for a chance to get into the big thing again. When I wrote last, I was in a forest that

This rolling kitchen prepared food for the soldiers that captured St. Mihiel. For lunch: beef stew, mashed potatoes, peas, bread, and butter. WHI IMAGE ID 71953

we captured. Perhaps you have read about Fritz's camp in the woods, where he was rudely surprised and chased out.

We can hear the roar of guns almost constantly, though they are quite a ways off. This is a rather cool morning and a fire feels comfortable. We are feeding pretty good. Of course, you know it is just plain food now, but we get plenty of it, and it is good.[46]

When Otis O'Brien was transferred from the 32nd Division to the First Division, he was able to get a position driving a truck with a supply company. It wasn't his job to go "over the top" into a line of machine-gun fire. He more easily managed to avoid getting killed or even wounded, and his letters home gave a relatively upbeat account of the activity of the First Division on the line of battle. O'Brien wrote home on July 26.

Dear Mother,

I feel guilty for not writing home the past two weeks, but if you were where I am you could forgive me. The news of the big drive here will probably be old stuff by the time this reaches you, but it has been pretty lively for the past two weeks here, and it is still going on as the lines are advancing. More than once the last two weeks I have sat at the wheel of this old truck for 36 hours and am getting so that I don't need much sleep.

They sure have to hand it to this old division for what it has done the last month. The Germans were headed for Paris when we thought we were headed for a rest camp. Instead of that, it turned out that we gave the people of Paris the rest by stopping the Deutsche. We did not know exactly when the boys were going over the top, but we had a pretty good idea. For two days and nights we were sure busy and the next morning we knew something had started, from the sound of the guns, and by nine o'clock the prisoners were coming in by the hundreds.

The second day we saw hundreds of cannon taken from the Boche. There is so much to tell of what I saw that I only wish I could sit down and tell it, instead of trying to write it. I was put on detached service at the hospital to haul wounded and hardly stopped my engine for 36 hours. It was not so bad until we started to haul litter cases and then we had to drive so slow I could hardly keep awake. I thought I was all in from lack of sleep and one of the doctors told me that I could quit the job, but he said they needed every truck they could get, so I stuck it out until we finished. Here is where the Red Cross is right on the job.

I did not see Paddy, Frank or Carp (Weisser, Milbrandt or Christensen), but I saw some of the boys of old Co. M. I received your letters with the pictures in them and they sure

look good to me. I had a long letter from Lyle [his brother]
and he is getting along fine; I know about where he is now, but
we are a long ways apart. I was where he is about the time he
hit France. There are a lots of things I could tell you, Mother,
but it will make another letter when we get settled again, and
don't depend on the [*Brooklyn*] *Teller* and forget to write because I haven't received but three since I have been here.

We all expect to see the beginning of the end of this thing
now that the Boche offensive has been checked, and things
look pretty good to us now, so don't worry any, but think of
the good times to come when it is finally over with.[47]

O'Brien had been promoted to corporal when he wrote again
on September 18.

I suppose you were as surprised as Fritz was when we broke
out on him in a new place. I am quite a ways into what has
been Germany for four years, and this has been a rest sector
for Fritz. He has everything fixed up like he intended to stay
here forever. Even the trenches are of concrete and the dugouts are like summer homes, they even have electric lights.
This is nothing like Soissons, and Fritz was taken by surprise.
He had all he could do to pull stakes and beat it to the rear,
burning everything he could.

I have been in several of the towns he has left, and some of
them are shot up where the Boche showed any signs of fighting, and others are not hurt at all.

We are having some real good weather again after all our
rain, and it sure helps us out with the trucks because the
roads across where the trenches were, were pretty soft and
were more or less shot up but are all fixed up now.

Fritz did not show much fight and the prisoners were glad
to be out of the war. I believe Fritz has lost his push, and from

now on will be on the defensive. I hope the next drive will take us clear to Berlin, but we won't have to go that far.[48]

He wrote again on October 4, 1918, in a letter addressed to his mother:

You are pretty well posted on what happened around St Mihiel and it was a real party beside what we have been through. The old French civilians in those towns were sure a happy bunch. Well, after we cleaned up that place, we were just in time for another crack at Fritz and we have broke out on him in a new place. I have been right up to the front lines several times, and they sure are making good headway. Speaking of prisoners, I have seen half the German army, I guess, and they are the luckiest bunch in the war.

This group of German prisoners was captured by the 32nd Division in early October 1918. WHI IMAGE ID 132724

I was coming back from the front the other day and was dodging shell-holes in the road, kind of looking over a bunch of engineers who were passing, and I saw Boyd Smith. He hardly knew me at first; I walked along with him a ways. Maybe I will see Lyle [O'Brien] up here someday, too. I am always on the lookout for him.

I suppose Albert [Weisser] is back there by now. I have not seen him since we separated, only for a minute or two. Hope he is not hurt so that he will not be able to use his arm any more. He can probably tell you a lot more about how things are over here than I can write. The news that Bulgaria has quit seems to be the truth now and that ought to make some difference. I don't see how the Boche can hold out much longer. We all hope it will soon be over with, but hope they realize they are whipped good and plenty. They have been doing some pretty dirty work on this front, to the wounded and they are paying pretty dearly for it now. They have left towns so badly ruined that you would hardly imagine it had ever been a town.

With lots of love for all,
Otis[49]

CHAPTER FOUR

Casualties and Illness

Many of the letters, of course, were not written from the front, but rather from the hospitals. The Americans fought for a relatively short period of time, but casualties were heavy. In the 32nd Division, 2,660 soldiers were killed in action or died of wounds; far fewer died of disease, drowning, or unspecified causes—about 450. Nearly 11,000 were wounded in action.[1] Casualties were higher in the First Division—organized as a division of 28,000 men, it suffered more than 23,000 casualties, including nearly 5,000 killed in action, more than 17,000 wounded, and an additional 1,000 missing or died of wounds.[2] Overall, during weeks of active combat operations from the end of April 1918 through November 11, about 60,000 Americans died in battle and 206,000 were wounded. Another 60,000 military personnel died of disease such as the Spanish flu. Half of those who died of disease died in training camps in the United States.[3]

LETTERS FROM THE HOSPITALS

Letters written from the hospitals tended to say similar things: "Don't worry about me." "I hope to get back to my company soon." "They are taking good care of us here and the nurses are

wonderful." The following letter from Wilbert Murphy, dated
October 8, 1918, is typical:

Dear Mother and all;
   I presume that by now you know I have been wounded.
You must not worry about me though, for it was just a slight
wound in the left knee. I can get around fine now and don't
expect to be here in the hospital very long.
   We were surely making it hot for Fritz this last time, let
me tell you. The morning we started it was still dark and there
was a heavy fog so that one couldn't easily see the fellows
near him. Just the second we started, our barrage opened up
on them and all you could hear was the crash of our shells
exploding. Occasionally one or two would come over from
Fritz, but that didn't stop us any.
   I got hit the second day about noon and then it wasn't
long till I got back here. Things look pretty bright now, don't
they? I hope the papers have the right dope.
   You mustn't worry about me not getting along OK because I'm feeling good, and these people at this hospital
surely treat us nice. The Y.M.C.A. gave us hot chocolate at
the "first aid" and at all the stops on the way back either the
Y.M.C.A. or the Salvation Army or the Red Cross had something for us to eat or drink.
   You can still send my mail to the company as I expect I'll
get back there soon.
      With lots of love,
      Private Wilbert Murphy[4]

Some of the letters were more explicit about how they were
wounded, like this one from Corporal Burdette Purdy of Company H, 127th Infantry.

I was wounded the 31st of July in the right upper thigh, the bullet going through and coming out through my canteen. On the 3rd of August I was on the operating table, but now I am feeling fine. Can walk a little but am still quite weak. In a few weeks I hope to be back with the boys again just as good as new. I sure was lucky for when I fell, they were hitting the hill like rain; and how I escaped at all is more than I understand. You see we were advancing against positions held by machine guns and the Boche were trying to stop us by shelling the hill.

Shortly after I was hit, I attempted to crawl for shelter and the only thing that saved me was a ditch. After dark, I crawled back to first aid, for there were lots who needed carrying worse than I did. I met some fellows from Racine at the dressing station and they couldn't do enough for me. I am in Base Hospital, No. 26 now, getting the best of care and I am doing fine, so don't worry, as it is nothing serious. Write often."[5]

Purdy was released in time to get back to Company H for another battle at the end of October, where he was gassed and sent to the base hospital at 59 Romancourt till December 14. He was then transferred to Tours and was doing okay until he suffered a relapse. The *Independent Register* reported that Purdy saw Warren Niles before he left the base hospital.[6]

Sergeant Warren Niles worked with the Headquarters Troop of the 32nd Division, and he had an unusual injury. In a letter to friends, he described how he was pinned under his horse for a couple of hours.

It was during the first days of the last drive that I got caught in a heavy barrage while coming back from battalion headquarters on my horse. I saw it coming and tried to keep in front of it, but a "155" hit about ten feet from me and knocked the horse and me about seven feet and when I came to, the horse was dead laying upon my leg and no one was near me so I had to lay there during that barrage before anyone came to give me a lift. But I am now in a hospital and feeling fine with fine care. But those two hours I lay there, sure made a difference in my life. I thought about everything that I ever did.[7]

When Sergeant Einar Johnson wrote to his sister on September 26, he had been in the hospital a couple of weeks already. He wrote, "I am getting along fine but I guess they are going to keep me here for a while. I will have quite a scar on the top of my bean. The bullet fractured my skull and they had to operate on it. I was going to save my helmet but I threw it away. The bullet went right through the top of it." He wrote to his mother about a week later and noted, "I am helping around the ward now. They have movies in the mess hall quite often and last night there was a vaudeville

Lieutenant Harry Humphreys entertains wounded men at American Evacuation Hospital #114, Fleury-sur-Aire, France, October 8, 1918. WHI IMAGE ID 132650

show in the Red Cross hut. This helps pass the time away. There are three other fellows from the company here besides myself."[8]

When Johnson wrote to his brother on October 18, he had been in the hospital forty-eight days and had yet to receive mail. He wrote a bit about what he had been through.

> I was wounded at Soissons. We went over the top at four o'clock in the afternoon and I got hit about a half an hour later. You should have seen the aeroplanes. There were over a hundred of them flying at the same time. I never expected to get out of Château Thierry alive. The Boche had control of the air there. We were relieved at Fismes and they were shelling the town when we went through. I'll tell you all about it when we get home.[9]

Johnson was still in the hospital on November 27 and had spent four months with no mail. He told his father not to try to send any more mail because he expected to be home soon.[10]

Some of the boys were in the hospital for reasons other than war wounds. Ray Olson, from Brooklyn, was away from his field artillery battery and in the hospital a couple of months, July and August 1918, with an attack of appendicitis.[11] Frank Milbrandt, also from Brooklyn, spent some time in Field Hospital No. 3 with the mumps. On December 18, 1918, he wrote, "This is my third day with a swollen jaw, otherwise I am fine and well."[12] He stayed in the hospital at least through Christmas. He wrote to his sister, "Merry Christmas! I am still holding down a bunk in the hospital, but hope to be out within a week. It sure is a tiresome job to lie in bed and still be in the best of condition only for a swollen jaw."[13]

Corporal Russell Agnew was with the Signal Corps of the 127th Infantry. He was wounded in early October at Verdun and spent four months in various hospitals. He wrote: "It was on October 4th that I was wounded and sent to the hospital. I found myself in a hospital about forty miles back of the lines. There for several hours before loaded on a French hospital train and sent to Base Hospital No. 15 at Charmont where I was treated for a week and then put on the American hospital train and sent to Base Hospital No. 38 at Nantes, where I remained till November 26." At that time he was moved to another hospital and was finally discharged on February 8.[14]

From the base hospital at Nantes, Agnew wrote several letters. In one to a friend, he said, "First of all don't start in and picture me with a leg or arm off when you see my above address. I have both of the above mentioned articles and their mates, thanks to the poor aim of the Hun." He described the hospital as a large one, not far from the sea. He noted that he had been downtown to see the city.[15]

In a letter to his parents, Agnew mentioned meeting a nurse from Madison and how nice it was to visit with her. He wrote about another patient that he was spending time with, "an aviator [who] was just landing when he saw a plane coming down, and right for him. It was on fire, he couldn't get out of the way and it lit right on top of his plane. Before he could get out, he had his clothes burnt off and his hands badly burned. He tried to save the two boys in the other plane for they were pals of his, but could not. They were burned up, and it has left him nerve shocked."

He wrote that he would love to be home for Thanksgiving, but

> We can be thankful that I am alive for I have had several close calls. I was on the Alsace front, was in the big drives at Château Thierry, Soissons, Juvigny, St Mihiel, and was at Verdun two days when they sent me back here.
>
> At Juvigny we had a hot time of it. One day a boy and I were putting in some telephone wires and a big shell hit about one hundred yards from us and threw us into the air

and we landed stunned in a small trench. When I came to, I sure did move up that trench on my hands and knees and so did the other chap. We went back and put in our line just the same. We looked as though we had been through barbed wire as I had six machine bullet holes in my clothes. That day our names were sent in for a citation and we each received the *Croix de Guerre*.[16]

Agnew wrote again on November 10 and mentioned that he had not gotten mail in over two months. "I worry for fear you are sick. We are a changed lot of boys since going through this war, for we have been pretty close to death and it has made boys pray who never did so before. I can tell you it is an awful feeling to have a shell burst near you and hear another coming and feel it is your end."

He continued, "I am coming along fine and I expect I will leave here soon, as I am back in the tents now and will go before the board soon and be classified. The weather is cold now and we feel it after being in the heated hospital. Our tent holds about seventy-five cots. We get four blankets, but I sleep with all my clothes on just the same. Write soon and do not worry."[17]

Elmer Swann of Brodhead also spent many months in the hospital. His parents had already lost one son in this war. Lee Swann enlisted about the time Elmer was touring New York City. Lee was at a training camp in Vancouver, Washington, when he died of pneumonia on April 24, 1918. The *Independent Register* published several letters from Elmer in May and June describing his early impressions of France. In each of them Elmer mentioned his brother, already dead by the time the letters appeared in the paper: "Give me Lee's address, I'd like to write him. Glad he enlisted." "Don't worry about Lee, because he is always O.K. and would write if anything had gone wrong."[18]

Elmer had also written from the front to describe the rats
and the countryside destroyed by war. When he wrote again in
mid-August, he commented on his work. "Our medical work is
very interesting. Sometimes our dressing station was an old cellar,
sometimes it was just where we happened to pick out, put up tents
in a sheltered place, and hung up our medical belts."[19]

On September 25, the *Independent Register* published a note
that his parents had received word that Swann was recovering
from a shot in the arm. The note quoted a letter written with the
help of a hospital nurse:

Can't write as I have been hit in the arm with machine gun.
Bone is fractured so will be in hospital a long time. Am in an
American hospital in Paris. I am getting along fine. Surgeons
and nurses are of the best and doing everything possible to
make a fellow comfortable. Was hit while fighting just north
of Soissons. The other boys are all right. Victory is coming
and coming fast. An old French nurse is writing for me. Give
my love to everyone.[20]

In late October, Swann was moved to a hospital at Ellis Island,
and later to another at Cape May. Toward the end of 1918 he
wrote from Cape May.

Dear Folks at Home:
      I received your most welcome letter several days ago an-
nouncing that box for Christmas. I am feeling better every
day, not only my arm, but in spirits, body and every way. I use
my arm now and then in eating, but it gets tired if I work it
much. But it's a lot of satisfaction to know that a fellow is on
the right road and riding at top speed. It is awfully awkward,
though, at times when you want to do something snappy, and
have to diddle around with just one hand. At the table when

a one-armed fellow eats, he has to lay down his bread, or fork
or knife, or whatever he has in his hand when he wants to
pick up a cup or reach for a plate. However this misfortune is
offset by the pleasure we have of sitting down with girls. They
always insist on doing all the waiting on you, and sometimes
will never allow us to use even the well member.[21]

Another letter written on New Year's Day reported on the
progress of his arm:

As to my bum arm, I would say that it is getting better and
better all the time. I can bring my arm up over my head now
by its own strength and twist it about considerably. It still
gets tired easily and makes me restless at night, but it doesn't
wake me at four o'clock in the morning as it used to when I
first came back. The biceps are stretching gradually so much
that one of these days you will get a letter saying "the arm
is straight, not crooked anymore." In my hand I can feel
something like electricity shooting down thru my fingers, a
good sign, because that means the nerve is improving. Slow
but sure is about the plainest way I know to tell you how it's
coming.[22]

Swann returned to Brodhead for a visit in late February, but
the arm was "not yet sufficiently healed to permit of his discharge."
He was finally discharged at the end of May, 1919. The report on
his arm at that time was that "he has regained the use of his right
arm to some extent, though it is still weak, and will probably give
him trouble for some weeks."[23]

Of course many died in the hospitals in France. Mae Howe
was a nurse at the US base hospital at Limoges who wrote a few
letters published in Brodhead's *Independent Register*. She wrote
of an American cemetery just outside town where thirty-eight

American soldiers attend to the grave of a fallen comrade near Juvigny, France, September 1918. WHI IMAGE ID 132730

soldiers and one nurse were buried as of September 10, 1918. She explained, "Each hospital takes care of its own graves. We have a slush fund. Each nurse gives five francs—about $1.00—each month, and a certain sum is used to decorate our graves." Howe noted that her roommate "had a dear boy out there. The fellow in the trench back of him was cleaning his gun when it went off and shot him in the back. He had to be operated on here on his arrival and hemorrhaged several times afterwards and died. He was so nice and was one of her first cases. She thought so much of him."[24]

Howe wrote of the "wonderful etchings" done by "one of my boys," and she told how the nurses liked to have little parties for the troops. On one occasion they made chocolate ice cream and served doughnuts and good coffee. She explained, "Our boys are simply wonderful. When you see them here: rich and poor, edu-cated and uneducated, all on an equal footing, and going through so much, it makes you feel so insignificant and useless."[25] Clearly the nurses got quite attached to many of the sick and injured for whom they were responsible.

When Leonard Rhyner of Monticello died of pneumonia at an army base hospital in France, a nurse wrote a moving letter to his mother:

Dear Mrs Rhyner:

I know by the time you receive this letter you will have been informed of your son's death over here, and I felt that you would want to hear some particulars. There is nothing much one can say in times like these to make your sorrow any easier to bear, but I hope it will prove a grain of comfort to you, at least, to know that your son was warm and comfort able and that everything possible was done for him all during his illness. He was only sick a few days, and during that time we all grew to love him; he was so sweet and good and did everything we wanted him to. I'm sorry I can't give you more particulars as to where he came from to this place. He was so sick we did not bother him with questions. I imagine he was sent here from some evacuation hospital closer to the front.

I am on night duty at present, and during the last night he lived I asked him if he'd like me to write to his mother and he said: "I wish you would; I'm afraid she'll worry. I always wrote twice a week. Tell her I'm feeling fine." He was delirious excepting when we spoke to him and didn't seem to suffer at all. This form of pneumonia just seems to be all through their system and the patients don't struggle for breath, but just run a high fever and are delirious until the heart gives out.

It really is heart-breaking to us nurses to see such fine young men taken as your son was, and you and all the rest of the wonderful American mothers, who are bravely giving their sons to their country, have all our sympathy.[26]

THE SPANISH FLU

Leonard Rhyner died in mid-October 1918, and while there is no
confirmation that his pneumonia was a complication of Spanish
flu, it is very likely. At least 20 million people around the world
died of the flu in the summer and fall of 1918. The disease spread
rapidly with the movements of troops for the war effort. Although
the vast majority of those who caught the flu recovered, 10 to
20 percent developed a deadly pneumonia. Ironically it was the
young adults, like Rhyner, rather than the old, that were most
likely to die.[27]

A milder wave of the flu had swept through Europe in the
spring of 1918, so when the more deadly strain returned in the
fall, many were immune. In the fall of 1918, however, the Spanish
flu was wreaking havoc in military camps throughout the United
States. At Camp Grant, for example, in Rockford, Illinois, just
across the border from Green County, some four hundred soldiers were taken ill by the third week of September. By October 9,
Brodhead's *Independent Register* reported that 262 men had died
from the flu at the camp. And the disease was not confined to the
camps; it was also sweeping through America's cities and towns.[28]

On October 10 the state health officer in Wisconsin ordered
all public institutions closed; schools, churches, theaters, saloons,
and public gathering places were closed until the incidence of the
disease subsided. Thus while the war in Europe was in its final
month, news of the flu epidemic at home was flooding hometown
papers, and letters sent overseas to soldiers contained reports of
friends and relatives who had been sick or who had died.

Since the young men were away, many of those who died of
the flu in the cities and towns of America were young women. For
example, the obituary of Clara Peterson appeared in the *Brooklyn
Teller* on October 31, 1918. Peterson was twenty-four years old
and a teacher in Brooklyn. She had studied music in Stoughton

Stories of the flu at home in Wisconsin competed with war news in the final weeks of war. *WISCONSIN STATE JOURNAL*, OCT. 10, 1918

before taking the teaching course at Whitewater Normal and graduating in 1916. Brodhead also lost a young schoolteacher to the Spanish flu.[29]

The letters from the boys contained mentions of the flu epidemic at home and abroad. Harold Thompson of Brooklyn spent his time in the navy on a transport ship taking other servicemen back and forth across the ocean. He wrote about the flu on his first voyage to France in late September 1918. "We lost 78 soldiers, 2 naval officers and one sailor, and left a number sick in France. The dead, we buried them, except the crew, which is always brought back to the States. I was lucky enough to pull through without getting it." The ship carried about eight thousand soldiers in addition to a crew of eleven hundred. Thompson also expressed his concern for those at home in Brooklyn.[30]

After the armistice many of the boys wrote home inquiring after the health of their family and friends. Charles Bontly of Monticello wrote to his aunt and uncle to express condolences for a cousin's death. He added, "The flu casualties in the States must certainly have been terrible; much more so than over here. In fact, we had very few cases in our outfit." Lyle O'Brien wrote, "I was surprised to hear of Clara Peterson's death. We had the same thing over here before it got there, but there is none here now."[31]

Wisconsin was better prepared than most states and waged an effective campaign against the disease, with a lower death rate than the country as a whole. Nevertheless, after subsiding around the end of October, the disease returned in a second wave in late November and into December, when schools and other public places in many communities closed again. In Wisconsin, 8,459 people died of Spanish influenza and related pneumonia complications. No county was spared; 69 people in Green County died of the flu.[32]

CHAPTER FIVE

⌐∿

Germany Concedes

An armistice ended the fighting on November 11, 1918. Communities back home celebrated long before letters about the armistice began arriving from the boys overseas. Indeed, the *Brodhead News* announced the end of the war on November 7, 1918, four days before the armistice was signed. Monticello heard the erroneous United Press report the same day and staged an impromptu celebration. "Elderly people who had not jubilated for many years were among the most jubilant, and joy reigned supreme from every angle." The fire bell rang for hours and a big parade continued throughout the afternoon. The parade included three big logging trucks, a neighbor's old tractor, whose whistle was described as both joyous and deafening, and a "little Fordson tractor." Regarding the latter, the newspaper reported, "With the muffler wide open you couldn't beat it for real downright and unadulterated noise." The celebrations were repeated on November 11, when the armistice was actually signed.[1]

THE FIGHTING AND KILLING ENDS

In France the armies fought until the "eleventh hour of the eleventh day of the eleventh month." In the aftermath of the armistice, many of the boys had little time to write letters.

Major General William G. Haan, commander of the 32nd Division, congrat-
ulates his men on November 12, 1918, and instructs them on their next task
in the army of occupation. WHI IMAGE ID 132729

Einar Johnson was in the hospital when the armistice was
signed, and he was able to go into Paris the following day. He
wrote to his sister on November 13.

Dear Sister:
    Just after I got that letter written the other day, we heard
that the armistice had been signed. You ought to have heard
the bells and whistles and cannon. Everybody went wild.
    Another fellow and I went to Paris yesterday. It was a big
holiday and the people sure were rejoicing. I have never seen
anything like it in all my life. The French people were crazy.
Every street was packed so that traffic was impossible. You
just had to go wherever the crowd went. There were parades
all the time. The French would grab us and make us get in the
parade. We were kissed by French girls, women, and men. A

bunch of girls would form a circle around us and dance, and then they would all kiss us.

All the buildings were decorated with the flags of the Allies. They showed pictures of all the great men at the top of one building, and at that street it was impossible to get through. We tried to cross the street a few times but we were carried along by the crowd for over a block.

There were soldiers dragging German cannon down the street. One parade had a dead hog set up in front of the vehicles with a cap on and a coat around it, representing the Boche. It sure was a sight worth seeing.[2]

Out on the front, however, the arrival of the armistice was rather different. Otis O'Brien finally had time to write home from Verdun on November 19.

Dear Mother:

It has been a long time since I have written a letter. The past two weeks have sure been exciting, and I have been on the road all the time. It hardly seems true that the war is over, but we knew it was coming, ever since we started in on this front.

I will never forget the excitement there was around here the night before the armistice was called. I was on my way to the front with a load, and the country around was all lit and burning powder. The Boche left great piles of it along the road, and every flash would blind you for a while. An M.P. told me to turn on my lights, and I could hardly believe him. For the last eight months, we had learned to fear a light after dark because we knew it would be liable to get us in trouble. Not only would we get shelled, but we would have a chance of getting bombed too. But it is all over now, Mother, but the shouting. And the chief argument is, as to when we will go

home. Some of the fellows think we will not get home very
soon, but I still feel that we will be among the first ones to get
back. Here's hoping so anyhow.[3]

During that long spell when O'Brien failed to write, his
mother received a letter from someone else in France that undoubtedly pleased her to no end. A note from the editor of the
Brooklyn Teller appeared in early December, two weeks before
that last letter was published. The note explained: "The following
letter written in French and translated by Miss Ruth Hersey was
recently received by Mrs C.F. O'Brien. The writer is an aged lady
and Otis O'Brien with others of our boys made their home with
her a few days while in rest camp. She was a mother to them while
they were with her."
    The translated letter read as follows:

Nov 5th, 1918
    Dear Madam:
    I promised your dear son that I would write to you and I
will keep my promise. We have had many American troops
among us, and have had your son at my home. I think, My
dear Madam, that you will permit me to say that you have a
son who is very gentlemanly and polite. I will think of him as
long as I live, and I desire, My dear Madam, at the close of this
terrible war, that your little soldier will return, safe and sound.
    Receive, My dear Madam, a cordial shake of the hand. A
short answer would please me greatly. My address: Mme Vve
Mascime, Place de Laissue No. 6, Longeville, Meuse.[4]

O'Brien had been too busy to write because of heavy demands
for the trucks in his supply train and the need to keep each truck
working. He explained to his father in a subsequent letter:

The division received another citation the other day, for what
we did in the last drive; and our supply train also received one
from the general himself. We sure had to work some and not
having very many trucks, those we did have were on the road
day and night. I broke a rear axle on mine the night before the
armistice. Was to start near Beaumont near Sedan and when I
got to town, I found out that the war was over with.[5]

Those who were in charge of keeping the tanks running were
faced with similar problems. Sergeant Elmer Dixon was in the
301st Heavy Tank Battalion supporting the action at the front.
He finally had time to write home to his family on November 21.

Dear Mother and Father—
I am at last back of the lines far enough to look at whole
houses and towns again, but it does seem pretty hard to believe that the war is really over; it seems only a few days ago
the shot and shell were bursting over our heads. I wrote in
my last letter that we were going back for a rest, but we were
ordered back into action again. We had to stick it out until it
was over, and some considerable time afterward. To be exact,
we stuck it out until day before yesterday. I have lost track
of time—I don't know whether it is Sunday or Wednesday.
Our Lieutenant told me this afternoon that it was the 21st of
November and he said that the only way he could tell was a
memorandum of some kind he had just received from headquarters. I have not had a decent bath and only one change of
underwear since Sept 9th.
We were dated for our first show on the 12th of September near Baupame, but the Germans retreated so far that
we weren't called upon until the big battle started between
Cambrai and St Quentin. That was the breaking of the

Hindenburg Line, and it took nearly two days to run them
out. We were in the next four stands they tried to make, and
it crippled the battalion so bad we could not go farther. The
next few days we expected to go back for a rest, but we got
a lot more tanks from somewhere and some men had just
come from England for replacement, so we were ordered into
action again. But we never saw any more fighting except for
the big artillery barrages. The Germans were retreating so fast
that the heavy tanks could hardly keep up; then the order for
ceasefire came, so we called our tanks in.

We had three tanks that had been in the last show and
were stalled. To be exact, the engines had gone to pieces, and
the British refused to salvage them. So our little repair unit
had to go out and draw them in and fix them up. The Battalion waited for them at St Quentin until we got them ready.
Then the day before yesterday, we loaded all the tanks at the
nearest railhead which was St Uasse. I drove the repair truck
and we went through Cambria, Arras, and about fifteen kilometers this side of St Pol. I got in here yesterday, and I don't
know how long we will stay or what we are going to do. I only
hope I can get cleaned up again so I can at least stand an inspection. I must try to get some clean clothes soon and see if
I can find a Y.M.C.A. to answer about two dozen letters that I
haven't had time to write in the last two months.[6]

THE MARCH TO THE RHINE

Both the 32nd Division and the First Division were chosen to be
part of the army of occupation. It was an honor to be chosen. Only
two other divisions accompanied them, the Second Division and
the much-lauded 42nd Rainbow Division. These divisions, with
their artillery, followed the Germans back to Germany, beginning

November 17, in a march that lasted nearly a month, over difficult terrain and in disagreeable weather. Some days the infantry marched up to forty kilometers (twenty-four miles); more often it was about half that.[7]

Reuel Barlow wrote two long letters to his father describing the march to the Rhine and his new situation after the division arrived in Germany. The first of these letters was written on November 24, 1918, and published on New Year's Day in the *Monticello Messenger.*

Of course you know that I am with the Army of Occupation that is on its way to the Rhine. We have been on the way a week now, and the trip has been great in comparison to the life while the war was still on. When the armistice was signed, we were on the banks of the Meuse River, not very far from the front, and we were under the German guns. Then the war stopped, and we did not have to put all the lights out, but we built big bonfires to celebrate the event and everything seemed very quiet at night because we could not hear the guns.

We had been in the "desert" over two months and had not seen a civilian nor an inhabited house during that time. Nothing but ruins and rubbish. Then, on November 17, we started for Germany, with all of our equipment in trucks and the men riding on top of it. For about an hour we rode through the country which was all blown to pieces. Then we came out into green fields and good hard roads, which seemed mighty good. The villages were all empty, but there was a stream of civilians walking toward us all the way, and many returning prisoners who had been released from Germany. They all were very enthusiastic in greeting us. Farther on, we began to come to towns that were inhabited, and the light showed out of the houses through the darkness, making things look homelike and comfortable.

About midnight we stopped at the edge of a little town
and slept in the barns or in the trucks. I pulled my blankets
around me and went to sleep in the back end of the office
truck. The next morning was freezing cold; I got up early, and
some of us started a bonfire at about 5 a.m. We ate breakfast,
consisting of rice, bread, and coffee, and then started on
again. That morning we entered the city of Longwy which is
right in the corner between Belgium, France and Luxemburg.
It is a large city and is situated in a long, deep valley. The
country is as beautiful as I have seen anywhere. The Germans
had turned the city over to the allies the day before.

We started a hospital in a large hotel, built in 1914, completed eight days before the war began, and used ever since
by the Germans for a hospital. It is a mansion, with parks
and fountains and health springs. I slept that night in a room
and on a mattress, with electric lights and hot water in the
room and a toilet across the hall. Our office was the hotel
office downstairs. That day the American army was given a
big celebration and the town was decorated with bunting and
lanterns and flags.

We stayed there two days; then the hospital was taken
over by another hospital outfit, and we moved forward. Along
the way we saw large German bombing planes with double
propellers used for night bombing; we had heard a good
many of them before the war ended. The Germans left many
serviceable trucks along the way, and we noticed that they all
had iron tires. There were hundreds of wagons, guns, etc., left
as well.

We pulled into another village the next night and slept
on straw in a barn. That day we passed through the lower tip
of Belgium to Luxemburg. Everyone talked German, and
the Luxemburg people were mighty fine. We bought bread

American troops enter Luxemburg, November 21, 1918. WHI IMAGE ID 132559

and jam and beer in the village, and the boys and girls and women folk along the way gave us apples—the first we had seen since April.

Then the next morning, which was about November 22, we pulled into this town which is called Welferdingan, in Luxemburg, five kilometers from the capital city which is also called Luxemburg. Here we have our hospital in the castle of the Grand Duke of Luxemburg. It is his summer home and it has gardens and fine furniture and draperies. Of course, most of the furnishings are packed away. We can buy meals here at the restaurants and cafés, but they are not very cheap. A meal that one would want in America for Sunday dinner, with two courses of meat and potatoes, cooked differently for each course, costs about $1.50. We use German and French money now.

This country is wonderful. Great big farm houses and the fields and fences and roads and houses are all as neat and

clean as they could be. Some different from America. We have
been given passes to the city of Luxemburg, I was there day
before yesterday (Saturday) and yesterday (Sunday). I bought
some small souvenirs which I have sent to you. I have had
some good meals and purchased some real candy. The Germans, I guess, did not cut down on sugar like the allies. The
city of Luxemburg has streetcars and fine, big hotels. Its population is 250,000 and the people did not help the Germans
fight, for their army contains only 200 men. They dress more
like the Americans and the city is more like an American city
than any I have seen, and I have been in Brest, Dijon, Belfort,
Paris, Château Thierry, Verdun, Meaux and other small cities.
Of course, they are nearly all old-countryish and Americans
are quite a curiosity. They talk German and French and so we
"parlez" a little French and gobble off a lot of German. I have
met quite a number of people who have been in America—
one old gentleman who said he lived six years, from 1870 to
1876, at the Palmer house in Chicago. There are many people
who come to America and then don't like it after a couple of
years and return to their old country. One fellow had worked
a couple of years in a dynamite factory in Indiana and now he
is back here. I don't blame him hardly.

We will be here probably for several days yet, or until the
Germans get out ahead of us. Then we will go forward again.
The people here say that all the Germans this side of the
Rhine are pretty much French and that they will be nice to
us. Of course, we aren't mixing with them if they give us the
cold stare.

The weather here has been perfect—plenty of frost but
neither rain nor snow. I must close now and I hope this finds
you as well as I am, for I am in the best of health. I will tell
you more of our experiences when I get back, which I expect
will be about Easter time.[8]

THE WATCH ON THE RHINE

Barlow's unit crossed the Rhine on December 14. When he wrote again on December 24, his field hospital was in the village of Rengsdorf, northwest of Coblenz.

Twelve miles on the other side of the Rhine. That is where we are now, in a beautiful, large summer hotel, situated on a high point from which we can see the Rhine valley and river miles away. The hotel has steam heat, electric lights, pink wall paper and fancy hangings over the chandeliers. The walls are covered with many mounted antlers of a small species of deer, which are to be found in the pine and beech forests and stretches of underbrush that cover the hills around us. Living here is a great contrast to what we have been having during the past six months.

The village of Rengsdorf is a notable summer resort and has fifteen large hotels where tired Germans used to gambol on the green. In the hills which line the Rhine valley are little waterfalls and streams, and old, old cottages and hunters' shacks.

We are northwest of Coblenz. Our last stop was in a village called Niedermendig, twelve miles from the Rhine on the west bank. We left there on Friday, the 13th of December, and crossed the Rhine River at 12:30 a.m. Saturday morning, under a full moon that made the night seem almost like day.

The valley, north and south, was lit up as far as the eye could reach with thousands of small lights, which revealed factories and locomotives spouting smoke into the night. The river is about as wide as the Mississippi at Prairie du Chien. The entire valley is densely populated, judging from the twenty or thirty mile stretch we can see from here, and it contains village after village. As we passed through them after

midnight they were silent and dead, shutters closed and only
dim street lights burning. On every corner American guards
were on patrol.

About 1 o'clock we stopped on a narrow street in the village of Weis for the night. The only "military" place we had
to sleep in was the trucks. Several of us started out to find a
more comfortable bed. We found a house with the shutters
open and the lights shining in every room. The kitchen door
was open, and in response to our knock, we were ushered
into the front room, told to sit down, and given assurance that
we could find plenty of room to sleep. Then in came a coffee
pot steaming hot, some marmalade, and a plate of German
bread—black, heavy, coarse. We were surprised. The whole
family was up, and the mother ironing at 2:00 a.m. They explained that they could not sleep on account of the big trucks
going by on the pavement outside. We talked until 3:30 a.m.
The family had one son in France, a prisoner for two and
one-half years. Another son had been killed, leaving a wife
and little boy. One son remained at home, and there were
three daughters in the family, from 12 to 20 years old. Every
one of them showed their anger toward the Kaiser. Speaking
of America, one of them said, "America! Ach, that is a fairy-
land!" We slept on beds that night—two of us in a small
child's bed—and it was pretty fine. We got up at 8 o'clock,
came downstairs, found water, soap and towels laid out for us
and breakfast on the table.

This may have been insidious propaganda for the Father-
land, but I think it was just good, every-day sort of folks'
manner of being human. There are those kind of people in
every country. I guess the American Indians even had them.
Of course we realize that some of our allies probably wouldn't
have been treated as we were. Funny thing, too, the Germans

here say that America is what beat them, and yet they regard
the Americans as good fellows and not as enemies. I think,
however, it is because the American is sociable, democratic
and at ease in any place he is dropped. And, anyway, it is a
long way from Ludendorf to this poor family, which never got
as far as Coblenz once in two years.

We still operate the triage and advance field hospital as
we did at Château Thierry, Fismes, Juvigny, Montfaucon and
on the Meuse. The triage is an advance sorting station for the
front line troops. At present we are getting only a few mumps
and influenza patients. The real sick we send farther back,
keeping only those who can be returned to their companies
in three or four days.

Tomorrow is Christmas. It will be like any other day for
us, and yet it won't be like any other Christmas. A year ago we
were in Texas, expecting to leave for the coast any day. If anyone had told us then that next Christmas we would be living
in a large summer hotel on the other side of the Rhine, we
would have told him that Bull Durham smoking tobacco was
too much for his weak brain. But here we are; and although
we haven't had any mail in over a month or received November's pay yet, and cigarettes and Bull Durham are scarce, and
there is nothing to do but stick to army life on Christmas day,
it is not so bad. Two months ago we were head over heels
in mud and water and corruption. Now we are eating our
meals indoors; we have hot water and a full length mirror for
shaving; and waste paper baskets adorn our office. There is
inlaid pearl on the head of my bed; and the bathroom walls
are green and red. Some people have written songs over less
than that. We are all fine. Edwin [Reuel's cousin] has resumed
some of his theatrical stunts and all the world looks merry
and full of sunshine to him.

Barlow continued his letter on Christmas Day.

A lot of things have happened since I wrote the above yesterday. First, several sacks of mail were dropped off here last night and several more this morning. I received several bundles of papers from you, also several *Messengers*, which were certainly welcome. The Christmas package from Ruth [his wife] also came last night, and this morning your letter arrived with the family picture. You couldn't have sent anything better than that.

Another thing that happened last night was that it snowed three inches, and the trees and bushes are covered with it. It is a very beautiful scene—the forests and hills and the valley and little villages below us.

We had griddle cakes and syrup for breakfast this morning, which was quite a treat. We'll have beefsteak for dinner, which beats stew. The Y.M.C.A. sent us a little book of Christmas songs, and this morning all of us in the office began singing like we would in church. The "Y" also sent each man a small box containing a can of tobacco, cigarettes and chocolate.

Yesterday Getzlor and I jaunted up and down the hills here for six or seven kilometers, taking in a waterfall a couple of miles from here, and viewing several valleys that were very picturesque. The waterfall is twenty feet high. Nearby is another little stream which tumbles down a steep hill for nearly 300 feet. We climbed straight up several little mountains and then sat down on a rustic seat to rest, where other Americans have probably sat down in peace times when they toured Europe. This afternoon I am going out again for a plow through the snow. Exercise is one of the best things a fellow can get out of the army.[9]

CHAPTER SIX

Waiting to Go Home

The men assigned to the army of occupation spent several more months in Europe before they were able to return home. During that time, many of them wrote long, reflective letters. Some tried to tell their whole experience from beginning to end in several installments. Some reflected on the horrors of war, others recounted funny stories, and still others commented on how the experience might enhance their future. All the boys were eager to go home.

MARSHALL REFLECTS ON HOSPITAL WORK

When Charles Marshall wrote home in early January, he reflected on the medical work he had been involved with. He wrote to his mother from the village of Rengsdorf.

> I am working in the office again, attending to the mail carrying dispatches, etc. Getzlor and Reuel Barlow are also working here, so you see our old tent is strong in this place. Division Headquarters are here so there are officers galore. We have a new general as General Haan now commands a corps.

Members of the Medical Detachment, 127th Infantry, 32nd Division in Alsace, Germany, June 8, 1918. WHI IMAGE ID 132719

Our hospital on the front was the advance surgical hospital—only taking very serious cases that had to be operated upon immediately. All the rest were sent further back. We ran a "triage" or sorting station thru which every wounded man from our division or others were brought first. Then the doctors decided which men were to be kept, and which sent on. We had as many as 1700 patients pass through in twenty-four hours. I worked in the triage when it was in operation, generally night duty. It was at times advanced farther than the field hospital. Three teams of surgeons have worked without rest almost continuously for three and four days at times in our hospital, and the results they obtained were wonderful considering the conditions under which they worked. Remember all the shelter they had, generally, was a tent or an old building;

and they saved a great many lives that would have been lost had the cases been sent back further. Personally, it has been the most interesting year of my life. I have seen much of hell, and much, too, that was beautiful, and through it all have gained experiences that will always be invaluable to me.[1]

HAHN REFLECTS ON SOLDIERS AND LIFE AT THE FRONT

When Requartte Hahn wrote to his father at about the same time, he told several interesting stories that illustrated curiosities he had been pondering.

The Piano at the Front

The soldier is a funny person. Although his experiences have tended toward making him act a person years older when he had things to do, still he is as easily amused as a baby. You will hear him singing old school songs, playing school-boy pranks on his comrades, making little wooden windmills to fasten on the pup-tent pole. He seems at a loss to find something to do when no work of a serious nature is at hand.

As an instance, while on the Soissons front, a bunch of men were in reserve a couple of miles back from the front lines, well within range of the enemies' guns. The men, having nothing else to do, went down to a demolished town and came back with a piano in pretty good condition. They set it up under a tree and bustling around found a good player and right there I saw a scene that was not duplicated, I believe, in the field. While the gang was congregated around accompanying the player, the guns of our batteries and those of the Germans were beating like drums, interspersed now and then by the hum of aeroplanes and the far off rattle of our anti-aircraft guns.

The Germans, by way of appreciation, dropped the largest
bomb that night that has ever been our experiences to hear.
We thought the world had come to an end for a few seconds.
It sure was a great finale and right there ended the musical
program. Thereafter I was among those that took out a mem-
bership in the card club, and we confined our amusements
to playing cards in a dugout. The dugout, by the way, was
not boom proof, but you know it looks like protection. As a
matter of fact, it would have made a fine tomb. At any rate, the
Boche could not see our lighted cigarettes.

Nerves Get Tuned Up

While in the Argonne, just in the valley below the village
of Montfaucon to be exact, we were camped or rather had
our pup-tents between two hills. The hill in back of us contained some German long-range guns which the Americans
captured and were using. On our right were some French
long-range guns, on our left a battery of French seventy-fives,
and in front were our battery. We were nicely situated right
in the middle. The Germans shelled this place continually by
day and night. In the night their aeroplanes would come over
with their salt and pepper shaker and would season us well
and often. When they had their fill of this kind of sport, they
would separate, and, as there was a road on our left and right,
both packed with traffic, they had great sport bombing them
and making us lose some more of our sleep.

The funny thing about it is that we went to sleep after
the Boche let up his bombardment amid the roar of our own
guns, but just as soon as the first German shell came screech-
ing over we would wake up. It shows the way a man's nerves
become tuned up.

Life at the Front

We did not mind the life at the front so much; in fact, when we left the active front for a few days, we were always anxious to get back. By this I do not mean to convey the impression that we were great heroes. But the fact was that at the front every man stood on his merit, and every man had to look out for himself. The only restrictions were that he do the work assigned to him, as he saw fit. On the other hand, when away from the zone of advance, you must watch every step; you have several formal ceremonies, formations, and inspections to attend daily. There is no time that you can call your own from morning till night. That is one reason why the men would rather be at the front instead of in the so-called rest billets. And it is another reason why we hope it won't be long before we see home and all that the word implies.[2]

MURPHY REFLECTS ON SOISSONS

In late January and February, Wilbert Murphy reflected on the time he spent in battle. He wrote long letters to his family about the activity of the First Division on the front line, in a way that he was unable to while he was in the thick of it.

In one letter, Murphy wrote about his time at Soissons in mid-July 1918.

Very short notice was given to get ready to move and it only took us twenty minutes to get our packs rolled and get into the trucks. We went by trucks to the Bois-du-Compiegse, and what a sight that line of trucks made on the road. Strung out for miles, as far as one could see, were trucks. It seemed as though there were an endless number of them, all filled with

happy but expectant Doughboys, but we imagined something
was up.

We rode all night in the trucks and reached the woods
about daylight. That day we spent keeping out of sight from
the aeroplanes and doing our best to scrape up what "chow"
that was available. Some of us found a deserted garden with
plenty of spuds in so we were fortunate in that way. That
night our kitchens came in, and next morning we had a fine
breakfast. And we were hungry too. All the time we were
in the forest, the main road was just jammed with traffic,
troops, tanks, guns, trucks with ammunition and supplies.
There was any amount of everything necessary for warfare.
We guessed from what we saw that something was going to
happen, which was true.

In the distance one could hear the steady rumble, like
thunder, of the exploding shells and cannon. Somebody was
getting h—— at that time, you know Fritz was just being
checked in his last drive.

Late in the afternoon of the second day we got orders to
roll packs and be ready to move. It was just getting dark when
our regiment went out of the woods toward the front. This
was the 17th of July and the morning of the 18th found us still
dragging along just in rear of our artillery positions. All was
quiet and everyone was tired out. All of a sudden there was a
snap as if something broke and every gun in the valley—there
must have been a thousand of them—broke the stillness with
a tremendous roar. It seemed like one continuous roar as of
thunder. For a moment we stood still with wonder and then
with a cheer we rushed past the artillery and into position on
the crest of a hill from which we were to jump off.

The first wave of infantry started over when our tremendous barrage began, and we soon followed. For five days we
went forward, stopping now and then for a rest or to organize

through a living hell of machine gun and shell fire. At length
we came to our final objective, Berzy le Sec, and the night of
the 23rd were relieved by the French and Scotch. Of our company, what remained of the two hundred fifty who were in the
drive when we started, only about seventy remained. Some
had been killed, but most were wounded.[3]

Nearly a month later, Murphy wrote again to his parents,
describing those five days at Soissons in greater detail.

Dear Folks,
This is just a sort of summary of what happened to me
during the five days we were in action at Soissons. Now I
don't claim to be heroic at all—I felt just the opposite many
times during those five days—so this is just a brief outline
about what the fellows I was with did.
As I wrote earlier, we got into position in the support line
about 4:00 a.m. on the morning of July 18. Our artillery had
opened up with a crash, and the hills and valley behind and
before us resounded with the crash of high explosive shells
and the crump of the guns. It was a terrific drum fire and it
served its purpose to surprise the Jerrys.
After what seemed ages to me, although in reality it was
only a few minutes, we reached the line and dropped into the
shallow trenches to get our breath and also to get our rifles
ready. Bayonets were fixed, rifles loaded—ready to fire when
we should run across the Jerrys in our advance. I was a buck
in Corporal Butt's squad then and was right next to him while
we were getting ready to go over. We each rolled a cigarette
and started to smoke—it helped our nerves. In fact I am sure
it helped mine, for though I was rather weak in the knees, I
tried to brace up and be as brave as he was. We had all forgotten about being tired, even though we hiked all night. The

excitement was great though none of the fellows near seemed the least bit nervous. "Porky" Flynn, of Chicago, was about the most cheerful of the crowd, and he had been even more tired, I believe, than myself on that all-night hike.

Just as we were smoking, the Captain came along and gave orders to get ready to go over. He was an exceptionally fearless man, and that gave us all confidence. Soon the order came to go over and over we went. Just as we went over, the man at the telephone back of me said that over half of the German batteries had been knocked out by our artillery fire.

As we went over the crest of the hill and down into the valley, we saw the French tanks making their way up the opposite hillside towards the Jerry trenches. We kept going ahead about an hour and then we got down in some German trenches that were pretty well battered up. Here we stopped a while to rest and let the flanks catch up. Far ahead we saw the tanks, most of them still going ahead. Shells from Jerry were coming over now, and twice while I was looking over the parapet I saw a tank stop, rear up on its tail (as we said) and nearly go to pieces from the force of the explosion. A shell had made a direct hit.

Flynn touched me on the shoulder once and said, "See that bunch of Jerrys coming." I looked and imagine my surprise at seeing nearby a battalion of them coming without their helmets or rifles. They had surrendered to the men out ahead of us and were now on their way to the rear. That made us happy because we felt that there would be less fighting to do the next day.

Soon we moved ahead and about noon came to a road which was being pretty well shelled by the Germans. Here we stopped and dug in. The whizz-bangs were coming over fast and you didn't have to listen very hard to hear the 88's and 77's whine thru the air and light a short distance from you.

The WWI Sopwith Camel was a British biplane fighter, introduced in 1917. WHI IMAGE ID 11860

Some of the explosives nearly took my breath away, the concussion was so great.

So far, we had run into very little gas. We had been advancing so fast that Jerry didn't have time to use it anyway. However, we could go no further that day until our artillery moved up further—as we were nearly out of range. The aeroplanes were pretty thick, I think I counted sixty-five in the air at once when we started over. They weren't all French or American either—several were British and not a few were German.

At the end of the first day's advance we dug in along a road. It didn't take very long to dig a rather deep hole, either. The shells were landing pretty close and a hole was some protection from flying shrapnel.

Nothing but corned beef and hardtack to eat that day, and very little water. About darkness Fritz stopped shelling and for a few hours it was quiet. We improved our trench and prepared for a counter attack, which we felt sure would come, for the Germans were well prepared here.

You remember their last big drive started the 14th and we had helped stop their advance. Now the 18th we were pursuing them.

I got a little sleep that night but no rest. One can't rest when his nerves are all strung up and especially not when he is as close to death as I was. Some of my pals had paid the supreme price that day and we were all sad but anxious to get revenge—and we got it.

Next day about noon, orders came to advance. Packs were adjusted and over we went. It was necessary to expose ourselves very much in crossing the crest of the ridge—consequently as soon as Jerry saw us coming he opened up; and we had very little barrage of our own ahead of us. Double-timing over the crest and down into the valley we went. Gas was in the valley so we couldn't stop. A few adjusted gas masks on the run. Most of us didn't. We gained the next slope O.K. and without a single casualty. Then we spread ourselves out in a wheat field to await the signal for a further advance.

Jerry must have seen us enter the wheat field for his machine guns kept up a constant put-put-put, and we could see the dust rise where the bullets hit around us. I had a queer feeling once when I felt something slap against my pack. When I got a chance to look I saw that a machine gun bullet just grazed my helmet and hit the pack going through the mess kit and finally stopping in the handle of the small shovel I carried. I felt pretty lucky—I must have had your prayers at that time, else I would not be writing this.

At four o'clock we started to advance again. This time the machine gun bullets were hell. Some of our best friends dropped, but it only made us more determined to stick it out and get our revenge.

We went a couple hundred yards and hit the Paris-Soissons road and then an open plain which was fairly level.

The road was covered with dead Huns and not a few Americans. They had had hard fighting. The cavalry ahead of us had lost a great many horses and now there were no tanks ahead of us. Still we went on and with a cheer, a shout of defiance to the Huns, we swept across that highway and into the open field beyond. We had broken their defense and they were in retreat. Our line of skirmishers across that plain was beautiful—yes, marvelous. Nothing but Jerry's "G.I." cans bothered us now and he was throwing over a bunch of them now. (By G.I. cans, I mean high explosive shells.)

We crossed the plain, went down a hillside into a valley, and captured the town of Ploisy—but we could not stop even though we were nearly exhausted. My throat and mouth were just parched dry, my legs ached and my head swam from the concussion of exploding shells—but I couldn't quit. I kept up with my Corporal and we passed thru the town and up the next hill. We gained the crest of the hill when the machine gun fire got so intense and deadly that we had to stop and seek shelter behind the crest of the hill. Our company was there alone—the outfits on our flanks had not gone as fast as we did. It was nearly dark—getting near the close of the second day fighting. We lay along the ridge—shooting now and then in the direction the machine-gun fire came from. Butts and I were digging ourselves a hole when the order came to advance. We had to take those machine-gun nests by a charge. We did and such a cheer as arose from the boys when we made it! That and the sight of us coming at them with that cold steel of the bayonets glistening in the last rays of the sun made the Germans' hearts sink.

Then we saw a wonderful sight. Going down the road ahead of us, at a distance of about 300 yards, was nearly a company of Jerrys in full retreat. They didn't even stop to yell "kamerad" or take their guns or anything. They just beat it.

We let loose on them with our rifles and saw quite a number
of them drop. Then we had to stop and re-establish connections on our flanks.

Finally, when it got dark we dug in. Connections were
re-established and we prepared ourselves for a counter attack.
It didn't come, however, though all next day while we lay in our
little holes, the shelling was fierce. The aeroplanes were fewer
in number now, excepting that Jerry seemed to have more
planes up than we did. Still nothing to eat and no water. When
it got dark on the evening of the third day, I and a couple other
fellows went after water. We succeeded in finding some after a
couple of hours looking for it and ducking shells. Got back to
our company O.K. and found that a little chow had arrived. It
surely tasted good even though there was but a little of it. We
ate our food and then about midnight withdrew a few hundred
yards and waited for the signal to go over again next morning.

The morning came and after a little barrage by our artillery, we started over. We hadn't gone three hundred yards
when over a hundred of the fellows were laying on the ground
wounded or killed. The second wave rushed up and filled the
gaps in the first wave. In about ten minutes we got to Berzy
le Sec, our final objective. It wasn't really our objective, but
we were so badly shot up that we could go no further. Only
about seventy out of two hundred and fifty men were at the
final objective when we captured it.[4]

BARLOW PONDERS FUN, HUMOR,
AND GOING HOME

Reuel Barlow also spent time reflecting and writing letters. The
following letter to the editor of the *Monticello Messenger* was written on February 4, 1919, from Rengsdorf, Germany.

Two copies of the *Messenger* just arrived for Edwin and I. As a result, I am so filled with thoughts of home that I want to sit down and communicate with someone at home. As I wrote several postcards last night and a two-page type-written letter to my father, I will just communicate a bit with you.

I certainly enjoyed the many letters from the home boys in uniform which appeared in your issue of December 25. I can hardly wait until Stanley and I get together; then you'll probably hear shells whistling and bombs exploding and Boche planes buzzing and the whole war being fought all over again. I remember once seeing two veterans of the Civil War sitting in a room. When they started they were about ten feet apart. As their memories became more active and their enthusiasm grew, they kept edging toward one another until finally they sat with their chairs almost touching one another, face to face, slapping each other on the shoulder and pounding each other on the knee. I often wonder if we will ever get like that.

Fun and Humor

I have experienced more fun and humor during my six months at the front than I probably will ever enjoy during the remainder of my life, at the same time seeing more horror and going through more discomforts than I would know if I lived two lives as a civilian. I can enjoy myself for a whole evening thinking over some of the funny things that have happened over here.

One night at Montfaucon, just before we were relieved, the moon was shining as bright as moons ever shine. Very soon after dark the air was throbbing with aeroplanes, German and American. All of us who were not on night detail at that time sort of edged over toward a dugout. Pretty soon there was a "crump" and then another, and pretty soon we could hear the "swish, swish, swish," as the German dynamite drops came down through the air. During a quiet spell one of our men ran out in the open, with a little white flag, yelling, "nuff, nuff." On another occasion one of our fellows got up in the night and began swinging his arms wildly and yelling. When they got him woke up, he said he dreamed he was beating it across a field at night, a German aeroplane after him, and he with a lighted candle stuck on top of his helmet, and he couldn't put the candle out.

While we were at Avocourt, after three weeks at Montfaucon, we were camped near several companies of negro engineers who were constructing a temporary stockade for prisoners. One day a black angora cat (where it came from in that desert no one could figure out) started toward a big, shambly negro called "Nightingale." The negro began side-stepping and shadow-boxing, and exclaimed, "Git away from heah, cat, git away. Lordy, lordy, I ain't never goin' to get home nohow now." Another negro held up a piece of corn willy one day and exclaimed, "They is Hooverisin' in de states awright. They's savin' de po'k chops and sendin' us de grease." Another was quite a singer and his favorite ditty was "Uncle Sam Sho' Am Murderin' Me-e-e."

I had probably better not relate any more or I won't know when to stop. Ha! Like someone has said, "It is worth a hundred thousand dollars to me, but I don't want another nickel's worth."

Awaiting Orders to Leave

Just now we are all expecting that the order to leave will come before the end of another month, and that we will

go down the Rhine to Rotterdam and sail for the glorious
United States of America. You can imagine how we feel at the
thought of it. In two more weeks we will sew on our second
gold service stripe, meaning that we will have cast our orbs
over the European landscape for just one year. And it is nineteen months that we have been in uniform. The dope is pretty
strong here and no doubt before you receive this letter, you
will know more than we do about it. If we are released by June
it will come up to all my expectations, but this last rumor
makes me want to believe that we may be civilians in April.

Events here are of little interest. We are being inspected
every few days by everyone—from generals to majors. The
other day two colonels from the Inspector General's department inspected us. We have a fellow who is quite sim-
pleminded and is used as a sort of scullery maid around the
kitchen. He is a sad-looking sight at his best, poor fellow. Just
before the inspection, the mess sergeant told him that he had
better go out in the woods and not show up at inspection.
Jimmy went down in the cellar and hid in the coal bin. The
colonels, however, found him sitting on the pile of coal in
a corner and pulled him out. Jimmy's face was as white as a
sheet, in spite of the dirt that enveloped him. He finally explained that he couldn't get ready to pass the inspection, so he
just came down there to be out of the way. Both the colonel
and our major had to laugh in spite of the very serious (?)
nature of the affair.

Rengsdorf is crowded with soldiers. We can buy post
cards and near beer here. There is a "Y" which sells a few
cigars occasionally and it has a circulating library of about
twenty-five books for 1,000 or more men. Outside of that the
only thing of interest is the scenery, for the natives are failures
when it comes to being up and doing. The scenery consists

of a fine view of the Rhine and the Rhine Valley, and of numerous high peaks and deep valleys, and castles, both new and ruined, and also plenty of forest. The other day I walked for two hours through it. Finally I saw a couple of snow birds, called it enough, and returned home.

Yes, the good old days are gone. No more do we feel Fritz's iron rations; no more do our ears hear the whistle and bang of a shell, nor the soft purr of a Hun plane, nor the sawmill snore of a Liberty motor; no more are the skies at night beribboned from every horizon by powerful searchlights piercing the heavens; no more sleeping in the mud, or in a truck on a crossroads that is under fire, because your truck is stuck there; no more going without water for three weeks because you can't get water fit to drink, so you let coffee satisfy you; no more the shoddy villages of France for us, and their little "epiceries" and their "vin rouge"; not even cooties anymore, for the armistice brought their doom; nothing but near beer and our daily ration of corn willy and stew, and a wooden-legged German to look at once in a while. And so we just sit and sigh for the day to come when we can eat ice cream and apple pie.

I am hoping to celebrate the Fourth at home. You can expect to see the price of cheese go up when some of us Green County boys get back and attempt to satisfy our starving appetite for that article. Best wishes to everyone.[5]

PERSHING REVIEWS THE 32ND

On March 15, 1919, General Pershing gave the 32nd Division a final inspection at Dierdorf, Germany. Arnold Hansen described the event in a letter to his parents.

It was a rather tiresome job waiting on the field before he inspected the division. We were on the field nearly four hours.
After the review he gave us a short speech, thanking the division for their splendid work in the lines, and as a unit of the
Army of Occupation. He seemed to be pleased with our treat-
ment toward the Germans, and said he was glad that we were
treating them as friends and not enemies.

The General sure is a fine man. He showed himself to be
more with the soldiers than some of the officers are. After
hearing him speak one cannot help but admire him and also
feel proud of the fact he is our Commander in Chief. I almost
had to envy the Y.M.C.A. women as they had the chance of
shaking hands with the general; such good luck doesn't fall to
privates. But some of the boys can say that he talked to them
personally, even if it was bawling them out for not having
equipment fixed correct, a spot on their coat, or perhaps a
coat unbuttoned.

From what I can get from the officers talk, the General
was very much pleased with the 32nd Division. Some of the
boys thought he did not give us enough praise, but perhaps
they did not stop to consider that we are only a small unit in
this army, and it would not do to praise one division more
than the other.

We think there is nothing like the old thirty-second. It is
not the same division that went in the lines at Château Thierry, as most of those men are gone, and the division has been
replaced with new men. They get the spirit the old men had
and keep up the good reputation of the division.

Things are beginning to look more favorable in regard
to going home, and I don't think they will disappoint us this
time. If everything goes O.K., we ought to be back in the
good old U.S.A. sometime in May.[6]

GOING HOME

Most of the men from the 32nd Division, including Arnold Hansen, did arrive home in mid- to late May. Harold Thompson of Brooklyn was working on the USS *George Washington* as it transported troops home. He was thrilled to find Bernie Christensen among the thousands of men on board. He wrote to Bernie's parents who in turn gave the letter to the *Brooklyn Teller*. The letter was dated May 9, Hoboken, New Jersey, and read in part:

> Bernie sure gave me a big surprise. When we left France last trip we had 6500 men on, and most all were Wisconsin and Michigan men. Naturally I was looking for some of the boys among them, and for two days I looked and asked different ones but could not find any of them. I found a number from other towns that I knew, and one afternoon I was talking with a fellow from Evansville, and who should come along but Bernie. You could have knocked me down with a feather, for I never dreamed of seeing him. You should have seen us meet; arms around each other like a couple of girls. You can't imagine the feeling it is to meet someone from home in mid-ocean. I am quite sure he enjoyed the trip for I did my best to make it a pleasant trip for him but could not keep him from getting seasick.[7]

Otis O'Brien and Einar Johnson were also among the Brooklyn boys that made it home in May, in time to march in a Memorial Day parade. Albert "Paddy" Weisser, who was frequently mentioned in O'Brien's letters for his injured arm, was also there.[8]

Elmer Dixon from the 301st Tank Battalion arrived home in mid-April. He had the opportunity to stay on, as he explained to his sister, but it was not for him. He wrote from Camp Meade on March 23.

Monticello's boys are home to march in the Memorial Day parade, May 30, 1919. MONTICELLO AREA HISTORICAL SOCIETY

We got pretty good news this morning—the parade as far as they know has been called off and if everything goes well we can get out of here very soon. They are trying to enlist men of our battalion to stay in the tank corps permanently; and for the Liberty Loan business, they are trying to enlist 301st men to be assigned to certain districts in this next drive. I suppose they want the men just for show, or maybe to drive a tank in their parade—anyway they want us for three months—to travel all over the Union. But it doesn't interest me at all. The Red Cross, too, has been trying to get some 301st men to help them on some kind of a drive. It's all very well for those who want an easy life for the next three or four months; they will get their regular pay they are getting now, and will sleep

and eat in the best hotels, all expenses paid. If it had been
any other time of the year except spring, I might have been
tempted to take the trip. My one ambition now is to wear the
red stripe on my left arm (discharge stripe).[9]

Both Wilbert Murphy and Reuel Barlow arrived home somewhat later because they took advantage of opportunities to study
in France while they waited to go home. Murphy spent a few
months at an American university in southern France and arrived
home in July.[10] Reuel Barlow studied in Paris under the Army
Educational Commission. As he explained to his father, "The
government pays us our regular pay and $3.00 a day extra for
room and board." His studies lasted from early March through
mid-June. He arrived home in August, and by early September
Barlow had accepted a position on the staff of the *Wisconsin State
Journal,* a Madison newspaper.[11]

PART II

Letters from Roger Skinner

Roger A. Skinner left an extraordinary account, published in the Brodhead papers, of his experience in France. Skinner's story was unique is several ways: He enlisted with the US Army Ambulance Service and was the first young man from Brodhead to reach France. Thus, he began writing letters from France in the fall of

1917, even before the boys who enlisted with the National Guard reached Waco to train with the 32nd Division. Skinner served with the French troops and had much less contact with friends and acquaintances from Wisconsin than did most of the other boys. He was also twenty-six years old—older than many of the other troops—and had left a job in Chicago to volunteer. Finally, Skinner

Reims Cathedral in Reims, France, served as a hospital during World War I.
WHI IMAGE ID 126155

made a consistent effort to write interesting letters home, and his family regularly submitted them to the Brodhead newspapers. Skinner and his parents, Mr. and Mrs. W. R. Skinner, were well known in Brodhead, and this contributed to the popularity of the letters with area readers.[1]

The first letter appeared on the front page of the *Independent Register* on September 19, 1917, with the headline "Roger Skinner Now in Europe." The letter is not dated, and it seems to have been written in stages while he was aboard the transport ship. Normally the letters were published in the *Independent Register* about a month after they were dated. Skinner's subsequent letters follow without further explanation.

⌒

"BIG BLUE WAVES AND WHITE CAPS"

Atlantic Ocean, Hotel de Roll

Dear Family,

I want to give you a good idea of the trip and still not put
in anything that is apt to be censored, for the letter would
then be slowed up.

You undoubtedly received postcard and letter mailed before leaving so know about when we left. I can't understand
the secrecy for everyone in the harbor knew when we pulled
out, but "rules are rules" and the Lord knows there are a
plenty of them in the army. If the Germans don't get me, I feel
quite sure I'll be shot at sunrise some morning for infraction.

Many times in the past, I have talked of a trip abroad.
Well, you can believe me when I say, that my idea of comfortable travel is not in a U.S. transport. We sleep in the second
hold, about on the water line. The bunks are of canvas, swung
between poles, three in a tier. They are really fairly comfortable. The worst thing about the sleeping is the air. Very poor,
as you can imagine, with several hundred men and no ventila-
tion, except what comes down the hatch and is not absorbed
in the first hold, where the kitchen and mess hall are.

The food is really much better than we received at Allentown. Have a greater variety and good cooks. The bread is especially good. Rough fare, and would really taste a lot better if
we were getting plenty of exercise. Felt pretty rotten first few
days on board, as the vaccinations made me pretty sick, but
after my last para-typhoid injection wore off, I have felt fine.

It has been a monotonous and trying trip. Nothing much
to do except to lie around on deck. We are allowed to stay in
one place only a short time, however, which is perhaps a good

thing. We are allowed in the lounge and saloon for about an
hour a day. That seems sort of tough for there are so many of
us and so few officers. Also they have their state rooms and
we are not even allowed in our quarters during the day, except
on a special trip.

You see the whole trouble is that it is hard for us to realize
we are in the army. It makes no difference what your position,
education, experience has been. You are only a private and
stand no chance of being anything else, as long as you did not
select a medical course in college. There are many chaps on
board, my age and even older, who have given up a good deal
to do this thing, and it means a pretty big sacrifice at our age,
both in time and money. But when the real work starts, we'll
all be glad we came.

The trip has been exceedingly quiet. I had no idea the sea
could be as calm. Day before yesterday, however, it started
to rain and while it cleared off during the night yesterday we
rolled around considerably. It really was great sport. This old
tub we are on is only a coast steamer, and it sure can roll in
any sort of a gale. This is also its last trip I hear; really don't
think it is very sea worthy.

Was on kitchen duty a couple of days ago, and it was great
sport rolling around down there swabbing off the floor and
setting up tables. It gave us some good exercise and kept our
minds occupied all day. In the afternoon, when we were off
for a couple of hours, three of us got together with a lad who
plays a banjo and tried some "barber shop harmony." The harmony was pretty rotten I guess, but we thoroughly enjoyed
ourselves.

Yesterday morning the convoys, sent out to meet us from
the other side, came over the horizon. It sure gave us all a
thrill, for we had been expecting them. They were destroyers
and came almost up to us, then turned around and we kept

right on going. No monkey business about it with them. Then the cruiser and the destroyers, that brought us this far, whirled around and let out their speed and plowed through the sea for the U.S.A. Some sight! When you see something like that, it makes you glad that you are even a small cog in the machinery of war.

Yesterday afternoon went on the submarine watch. There are twelve men stationed in six different lookouts on the hurricane deck, with glasses, on the lookout for subs or anything else they may see. Each pair has a certain portion of the dial of a clock to look after. For instance I was watching from 10:00 to 12:00. It was a beautiful sight to be staring through the glasses out across the sea, and have one of the destroyers run across your line of vision—especially yesterday, for the sea was beautiful, with big blue waves and white caps breaking on nearly every one of them.

I think that covers the trip pretty well. We expect to come to port within the next two days. I may add some more before landing, but want to get this censored on board, so it can go back by return mail.

It is hard to tell what the next few months will bring. Don't imagine I will see any active service for several weeks though; probably will be kept busy putting Fords together.

I sure will be glad to get on land again and get in some clean clothes, take a good hot bath in fresh water, and put my feet under a regular table again. I fairly turn green with envy when I pass the staterooms. Who would have thought three months ago that one R.A.S. [Roger A. Skinner] would be looking for German subs off the coast of Spain or France, wherever we are. The things we have gone through thus far will seem like a vacation to what we will get later, but then we will have the hard work and excitement to keep us going, and a man can stand most anything if he is busy.

My life has been fairly rich in experience thus far, but am
sure this will be the climax. If it so pleases the Power on High
that I come back to you, I certainly will be thankful. If it's the
other alternative—well, the time comes to everyone, and as
Granny used to say, "You'll live till you die unless the Indians
carry you off."

Hope that we may see each other again before another
twelve months roll by. Please remember me to all friends at
home.

Love to all, Roger

Address me: U.S.A.A.S. [U.S. Army Ambulance Service]
Section 17, American Expeditionary Forces.[2]

~

"DON'T BE AFRAID OF FLOODING THE MAIL"

France, August 20, 1917

Dear Folks,

Sunday morning and if it wasn't for the fact that we have
no drill, it would be hard telling what day it was.

We are allowed to say that we are in France. Really don't
suppose that is any news to you; however, it is quite as picturesque as I had thought it would be. But of course the country
and the homes have not been kept up since the war started.

We have every other night off until 9:30 and generally go
downtown for dinner. We have lots of sport trying to make
them understand our combination of French-English gesture
language; but we manage to get what we want.

The money system is a bit difficult. Change a five dollar
bill and you get fifty-six francs. A franc is worth twenty cents
in our money, so we make a little on the exchange, but feel
quite sure the people make it up on the change. They are

very polite and courteous in all explanations, however. This afternoon, if it clears off, am going to try to rent a bicycle and ride around the country some. Everyone rides them here, especially the women. The women do most of the work and a great many of them wear black. It brings it all much closer home to you.

I received the letter you mailed to Allentown, about the time we left Thursday. A shout of joy went up when it came, for it was unexpected.

In a few weeks' time, after the news is old, I can write you in detail of the trip over. Think you will find it interesting; it was to us at least.

The food has been very good and am feeling fine. We don't know anything about our future movements. Don't be afraid of flooding the mail. When you send the cigarettes, you might put in some bandana handkerchiefs. Have to wash the white ones too often.

Love to all,

Roger[3]

⤳

"MAN THE BOATS AND STICK BY YOUR POSTS"

October 3, 1917

Dear Family,

Am going to write you something more of our trip over. There was really very little of an exciting nature until about two or three days before sighting land. One afternoon I was comfortably (?) curled up on the lower deck, lying on some deck hose in the sun, when the alarm was given for subs. Well it didn't take me very long to get to the life belts with the rest of the boys. One of the other transports fired a couple of shots and one of the destroyers chased over to where they thought they had seen the periscope. That was all, however.

The morning we were supposed to sight land, I was on the port bridge watch. Believe me I was looking for all I was worth, too, for the first signs of shore. Water is a great thing, but there are times when you've had enough. Anyway, I saw something that looked mighty like a shore line and was about to call to report it, when the whistle blew the signal again for subs. Then happened, what to me was a wonderful sight.

It seemed that in no time at all the transports had circled out, and the destroyers were playing around them like dogs around sheep. Then the action started. Believe me, when three-inch shells started to whistle around, I began to suspect there was something going on. Sort of like shooting fish; you see something and let her fly. In some cases the shells were whistling right close. One time our ship was given an awful shock, and the commander turned and shouted "We're hit— man the boats and stick by your posts." I had the glasses at the time and of course could not look around. Didn't even have a life belt on then. We were not hit, however, simply the jar and shock from throwing over a bomb. Well the whole affair kept up for an hour, most of it on the other side of the ship, worse luck, but I saw enough.

If you were to ask me whether I was frightened, I would hardly know what to say, but I do know I was so darned excited that I was as cold as ice. I wasn't worrying about not getting ashore, for by that time we could make land out plainly.

After the firing had been going on for about half an hour, we heard a loud humming noise, and the first thing we knew an aeroplane came by right close with the French flag. They cheered us and you can imagine what we did in return. After that, it was all better; but never was I so glad to see anything as I was that plane. I think also I would have given $10 for a cigarette while it was going on. I wouldn't have missed being on watch that morning for several months' pay. I saw several oil whales, one periscope, and one torpedo that missed us by a few feet. It made me mighty proud of our Navy for the way they handled it. So far, I guess from reports, it is by far the largest submarine engagement of the war. Of course the official reports will come out in time and give the dope on how many subs were sunk. A goodly number I know. This whole engagement was published in one New York paper, so we hear from men who have just come over.

We are working now from a base hospital right outside of Paris. Get downtown about once in four days. Otherwise we are kept in very close. This will do for this time and hope it will reach you soon.

Love, Roger[4]

⌐∽

"IN AN OLD COLLEGE WHERE
NAPOLEON III ATTENDED"

October 14, 1917

Dear Family,

Sunday morning and if I only had the Sunday *Tribune* beside me now, I would be almost contented and happy. I sent you several postcards the first of the week giving views of the place where I have been stationed this week. For fear they will not reach you, however, will give you a brief description.

The hospital is located in an old college where Napoleon III attended. It is beautifully located; and when the weather is good, it must be beautiful around here. The place is very old of course. Within a short walking distance, is a château over 300 years old, very much in ruins now, and the place used as

An American ambulance driver, Sergeant J. W. Killigrow, socializes with French children, November 4, 1918. WHI IMAGE ID 132648

a farm. Luckily my day to go up to one of the aviation camps was a fine one, and had a delightful ride of an hour before reaching there. The camp was of great interest to me. From there I made two good runs on towards the front and passed through some of the best looking country I have seen so far. The next day drove into Paris.

Outside of these two days, have had only little sunshine, it has rained most of the time. Joe Lee and I generally take a good walk after tea and go over to the best café in the village where the *blessés* (wounded) gather. It is run by, and is the home of, a very nice French woman and her two daughters. They are very kind and take great pains to help us with our French. I am getting so I can make myself understood quite well, and am grasping it better all the time. I think before the winter is over I'll be able to speak and understand it very well. It is difficult though, especially the understanding.

We have had excellent food and beds here and am beginning to pick up weight again. It really is a great experience, and certainly a liberal education. I am mighty glad I came and am more than happy to do even this small part for the French, for I have sympathized with them so long. Now that I am here, I like them tremendously.

Keep well and love to all,

Roger[5]

~

"A MIGHTY GOOD FORD"

November 25, 1917, Sunday a.m.

Dear Family,

Thought I would get an extra letter off to you this week, but here it is Sunday again before I hardly realized it. We had a heated argument yesterday whether it was Thursday or Saturday, so you see we don't pay much attention to the days.

I am writing this from a little hotel down the road from our hayloft. There is a fire here with tables and chairs and French hospitality. Got in at twelve o'clock from another 24-hour shift at one of the advanced posts. Had two runs up to the trenches and two evacuation runs back. That is the most anyone has had yet, as things are rather quiet just now.

An American ambulance
driver poses on the front
fender of his Ford ambu-
lance, ca. 1917. WHI IMAGE
ID 4587

The run last night was after dark and it is quite a stunt
to follow these steep winding roads without lights, passing
trucks and motors and sort of feeling your way along. It is
fortunate that things are quiet now, as it gives us a chance to
learn the roads under favorable conditions. Have a mighty
good Ford and am beginning to like it; it certainly does the
work up here.

We have been having exceptional weather for this time
of year; some bad rainy days since arriving but not especially
cold. We certainly are thankful, too, after what we had on the
trip up here. I am feeling fine again and eat like a horse. We
get plenty of food and our cooks can cook.

One place where we go there is an old National Guard
chef, who runs a café. We take our meat over to him (un-
cooked) and bread; and he cooks meat for us and throws in
some wonderful French fried potatoes and apple cake for 35c.
Then there is danger of our eating too much. The only com-
plaint I have is that it is hard to keep clean, living in a hay loft.
All my clothes are soiled, and I'll be damned if I'll wash them

in cold water. Did get a hot bath last Sunday, and oh boy, I
think I lost another ten pounds, and four shades of color. I
won't say how long it had been since the last one.

Sunday was a great day for us—mail and packages, all
I could carry. Sure that it was Christmas. Sweater, tobacco,
stocking cap from you and cigarettes, and box of eats from
Field's friends in Chicago. The sweater is a beauty and socks
are great—get some more if possible, and a pair of big heavy
mittens—just heavy and warm, not fancy or expensive. The
climate is very similar to what we have at home, so you see I
am in no summer resort, but, Lord with plenty of food and
ten hours sleep, I guess I'll get by.

When we get back from our shift we have to go over our
car and get filled up with gas and oil. Then we are off for the
day. Eat supper at five o'clock and call it a day after seven or
so. Get up at 6:30, fall out of our bedroom into our kitchen
and start the day. I have been out every other day until just
now and am off duty for two days now. I would much rather
be out every day though, for the time passes much faster, and
then feel that am doing something. Things are pretty quiet
now, but we can never tell how long we will be in one place.

Certainly have seen heaps of this country. Wish I could
tell you where I am now—am sure you would be surprised.
Also, if there is anything in the last rumor, we'll see a lot
more. Speaking for myself, I would rather see more work and
less country, but you go where you are sent and that is all
there is to it.

I saw some of the finest air work I have ever seen yesterday. But the very best sight of that kind was before we left the
other station. There the planes patrolled the city nights. One
beautiful moonlit night I was on guard, and one of the planes
with a light that looked like a large star, drove towards the
moon and dipped right across it.

Most good things seem to happen here on Sunday. Last week it was *beaucoup* (much) mail and this week we received our pay. By the way, I was made a first-class private some time ago, thereby increasing my pay $3.00 a month. I was quite overwhelmed by the honor. There are supposed to be 26 in each section, however, so it was quite general.

Guess that is about all, but I sure could talk an arm off you all if I had the opportunity.

Best love to you all and don't worry. I am happy to be doing the work I came over to do.

Roger

P.S. Any magazines will be very thankfully received as I have absolutely nothing to read.[6]

⁓

"THE CHRISTMAS BOX"

December 22, 1917

Dear Family,

Well, it came and I did it. By "it" I mean the Christmas box, and by "did it," I mean I opened it. I know it was very childish of me to do so, but you see we have got to move from our "home sweet home" pronto and was trying to pack and arrange my kit today. And then too, away down in my heart, there was that old, old feeling that everyone has sometime or other, the night before Christmas, and you just sort of want to sneak downstairs and see what you've got.

My side partner in work and I were on duty yesterday, and as luck would have it, Ed had the long runs. Oh, boy, it was cold! This morning, however, I got a run just after I got up; got back at 9:15 and had a breakfast of three fried eggs, crisp bacon, coffee, with milk, bread and jelly and mince pie. We got the food from some natives the night before, and our New York chef cooked it for us.

When we went to 1:30 roll call, they told me I had packages at the kitchen and I could hardly carry what I had with both arms. What more could one man ask! Your box was the last I opened and I sure did enjoy it. I was just telling about the time Pete Moore asked me who I was going to vote for, back in 1912, my first Presidential vote, and then I saw his name and Mrs. Moore's on a package. The lamp and extra battery are fine and it sure will come handy changing a tire some night about 11 o'clock. I may not be able to write them and the others, so please read them all this letter.

Know you would all like to hear something of what I am doing, but our Lieutenant is censoring mail now, and he would never get it off if he had to read every letter, so I'm on honor to forget the war in letters for the present. You read more about it than we can tell, and our work is pretty much written up. Sherman said it, but he did not say enough, for he had not seen this war.

Now, dear family and friends, I hope you have had as fine a Christmas as you gave me today. I know I won't have a chance to write on the 25th, and am making the most of a fire and a room tonight. You are all doing your bit, and I mine, and we act for the same great cause. Let us all hope and pray that the victory will come soon and remember whatever the cost, it was for the right.

Later—This morning had to make a run up, and guess the Boches thought they would open up a little for my benefit. Ran up to post, ran for a dugout, saw my man run out with his stuff and jump in, so out I went and without one lost motion, "little old Henry" and I went down the road. As long as they let me off with just a thrill like that I won't care.

Well, we are sleeping in a barn again as we had to move
a little ways. Christmas eve about ten of us walked over and
had dinner with our friend the New York chef. It was some
dinner. We then stayed on until midnight Christmas and it
was fine. They have a beautiful organ there. About the best in
the whole country and the finest I have ever heard except in
Salt Lake City. About the time I got to bed, you were at your
Christmas tree.

We have a pretty good place to eat in—a new building
we took over. Made one long table and one short, got some
green pines and decorated a bit. Had dinner at 3:30. One of
the Frenchmen had been up to Paris and brought back the
biggest turkey he could buy for us. Our Lieutenant ate with
us. After eating, our French officers came in and we sang. The
Lieutenant who has sung a good deal in opera, also sang. And
say, he has a voice! He has been in this work since the war
started, speaks French fluently and also was in the United
States Army in the Philippines. We certainly are lucky in
having him.

American ambulance drivers slept in their cars to be ready for the next day's
work, Meuse, France, 1918. WHI IMAGE ID 126156

Well folks, I told the boys I wanted a white Christmas, and when I woke up Christmas morning, the snow covered my blankets—sifted in through the roof. And it is cold, still zero and below and that is cold enough when you are driving two to four hours at a stretch. Hands and feet are the only parts that get cold though. Yesterday I bought a large pair of wooden shoes, with thick oak soles and leather tops. The size is 32 and they look like 50. However, with two pair of heavy socks and a pair of felt slippers they do the work.

It's a great life if you don't weaken.

Thanks and love to all, Roger[7]

⌒

"HAVE HAD TO GO OUT ON A GAS ATTACK"

February 7, 1918

Dear Family,

Haven't written for over a week now, but expected to go on *repos* (rest) yesterday, so thought I would save all my letter writing until then. We had the kitchen all torn up and were about ready to pack our cars, when orders came to remain here. There was to be a French section to relieve us but nothing doing—and we are now detached from the Army division and attached to this sector. It is really the most sensible thing, but we hated to leave the division, as we knew the men we worked with. When they go to another front, we would have gone with them. As the French sergeant says, however, after seeing all the fronts for three years, this is the best. They may change orders again tomorrow, so why worry.

Sure did get a fine bunch of mail today, about thirty letters. Also received the fur cap and other things. Thanks heap. Please put in an extra can of tobacco once in a while so I can

give it to my friend the New York chef, "Doc." Civilians can
hardly buy tobacco now. As they have been so fine to me, I
like to help with his tobacco supply.

Can answer your question about how many men go out
on a car. Only one now. If there is a real heavy attack, they
would probably put two men on. It makes it rather lonesome
for a man out on a lone post, but if there were two on a car
we would be out all the time. Don't know what the "cooties"
are, but if they are fleas, I have 'em. Not so bad now, had a
bath and changed all my clothes, but at night they still bother
me some. We are in hopes of getting better quarters soon,
but guess I can stand anything after the barn in the coldest
weather. I really think our real winter is over. Have a good
deal of fog now and it makes it bad for night work, but things
have been pretty quiet lately. They are probably giving their
guns a new coat of camouflage. Wish they would put silencers
and shock absorbers on them, for it is certainly disconcerting
to have one bust near where you are driving. One of the boys
was in the thick of it the other night. The lights on his car
were smashed and a piece of shell hit his helmet.

Am here at the office for the night. You see one man always has to stay here at night to answer telephone calls and
get the men up for the night calls. Two times that I have been
on call here have had to go out on a gas attack. The last time
we went out we had three cars. We picked up the guide about
half way to the place. He rode with me and I asked him to tell
us when we were into the gas. He said he would say "mask"
and then I should stop my car to tell the other boys. Well we
started, again, but had not gone far before I started off the
road through a hole in the camouflage. It was very dark and
I took it for the road. Well, we stopped the car and both of
us got out. As he walked back of the car he said something
that sounded very much like "mask" but he was only cursing.

We started on again and after going another half mile, picked up another guide. We then ran through a small town with narrow dark streets, and finally arrived at the place where they had the men. I turned my car around and then looked for the other two, but they were nowhere in sight. I started out to look for them, but had driven so slow I did not think it possible they could have lost me. I couldn't find them and was afraid I would get lost myself, so went back after one of the guides. We started out and finally found them. One of them had run his car into a small ditch and was having trouble getting one of his wheels out. They had their masks on and had them on ever since we made the first stop. It is practically impossible to see with the darn things and they smell too, heavens!! When they heard the Frenchman swear, they thought he was ordering the mask and didn't lose any time getting into them. That is one thing I have a horror of and would much rather take my chances with shell fire.

One of the boys, the youngest and quietest in the crowd, has received the *Croix de Guerre*. Not much formality about it. Those of us in camp came up to quarters and we all lined up with helmets and masks on and the decoration took place. Just a small crowd of Americans away off by themselves doing their work the best they can. He cannot keep it, belonging to the U.S. Army, but it was mighty fine, and everyone was mighty pleased that he had earned it. He is only 19 or 20, and I don't suppose he was ever 150 miles away from his home in Virginia before.

Tomorrow I go out on one of the hard posts and then hope to get a couple days off, for I have been on pretty steady for the past two weeks.

Hope the cold weather has moderated for you and that you have all come thru it without becoming ill or *malade* as we say.

My love to all, Roger[8]

⌁

"THE SIGHTS WE SAW WILL STAY WITH US"

February 25, 1918

Dear Family:

Guess I had better drop you a few lines while resting, for I have been busy, and am going to be busy for a few days. Folks, I could write you a very interesting letter today, if I knew just what I could say and what not to say. But I haven't asked the Lieutenant as yet, so guess I won't say very much.

Yesterday morning when I got to bed at nine o'clock, I had been going for over thirty hours without sleep and had only had four hours in the last twenty-four before that. I was in a third line trench *abri* (shelter) for six hours during a very, very heavy bombardment. Mostly French, but such a steady roar I never heard before, and never want to hear again. That was from 9:30 until 3:30. After that it was steady driving getting the wounded back to the hospitals. The firing lasted until about 9:30 that night and we worked right on until five in the morning.

It was a great experience, but I don't think I would want to go through it every day. We did, I think, mighty good work and the French *Chef* (leader) was more than pleased. However, we had many things in our favor: we knew the roads, the Boche shelling was not heavy, and there was a good moon. Nevertheless it was work, and nerve racking to say the least. Am glad to have gone through it, and mighty glad to get out of it, but it was terrible and the sights we saw will stay with us for a long, long time.

I slept from 9:30 until five in the afternoon and from ten until eight this morning so feel pretty good again. I sure would have given a good deal to have fallen into a tub of hot water and then between two clean sheets yesterday though. Will write a longer letter later and tell you more about it if possible.

Don't worry. I'm not, but believe me I will always vote for a sane and quiet Fourth after this.

Much love, Roger[9]

⁓

"PRAY, H——, I'VE BEEN PRAYING FOR THE LAST TWENTY MINUTES."

March 4, 1918

Dear Family,

Well, the mailman came today and while I received eight letters, they were all old ones and only one from you. But a letter is a letter these days, and they come only too seldom.

Things have been fairly quiet since last Saturday, but business in general all along the line seems to be picking up. Hard to tell what it will be here this summer and whether we will stay here or not. We know the sector very well now, so may stay right here. On the other hand, we received lots of praise from the French for our work last week, so they may take us on. Really makes very little difference to me, just as long as I can keep going and the victory isn't too far in the future.

Will tell you of an incident that struck us all as very funny. One morning one of the boys was bringing in his load of *blessés*, with one sitting in front with him. The Boches were shelling a bridge we had to run over. A large shell struck and exploded just to one side of the road opposite his car. The Frenchman said "*pres*" meaning close. The boy said: "pray, h——, I've been praying for the last twenty minutes."

That same night I had to go up about 5:30 to the most
advanced post. There had been heavy shelling in the morning
but it was quiet in the afternoon. When I had left this place
on the last trip about two o'clock, they hadn't gotten all of the
remains away yet. Felt rather leery of going up. When I got
there, found a little *blessé* waiting for me, and he spoke English. If I had been French, would probably have kissed him,
as I was so glad to find somebody speaking English up there. I
had a note I had to take down to *Post de Secour* in the second
line trenches. It was about twenty minutes walk, but had been
down there twice before that day, so had no trouble.

These trenches are like those winding galleries you find
at summer parks for five cents a try. Coming back I walked at
same rate of speed, I thought, and at the end of half an hour
was still going. I climbed up on top but saw nothing familiar
so kept on a while getting a bit worried. In about five minutes
more, I stopped again and still nothing familiar. I thought I
might be on my way to Berlin, so started back to *Post* for a
new start or a guide. I walked for about fifteen minutes more
and came to a cross trench, looked up it and saw a lighted cigarette. Said to myself, well here goes on the chance of a friend.
It was my little *blessé* waiting for me and say, it didn't take me
long to get out of there. Was in no danger, but in this case
ignorance was not bliss. This all happened weeks ago, and believe me I know all the trenches now.

This weather—there is about one or two feet of water
in the trenches and it is hard enough to walk by yourself. But
last Saturday I saw Red Cross men or stretcher-bearers coming along these same trenches on hands and knees carrying
wounded on their backs. I take off my hat to them. They go
over the top with the infantry and work out there in Noman's-
land for hours afterward, bringing the wounded in.

No-man's-land was the area of land between the two enemy trench systems, typically strewn with barbed wire. WHI IMAGE ID 132556

Guess this is as much as I have ever said about the war. At times, due to the sights we see, I am thankful that it is not our own boys. But just the same, I wish I were with them. Anything to put an end to it all.

Don't worry for as they say, the shell that hits you, you never hear.

Much love, Roger[10]

⌒

"THE FRENCH ARE CERTAINLY
A HOSPITABLE PEOPLE"

March 9, 1918

Dear Family,

Well, if it is as nice a day with you as with us, I imagine father begins to feel like making garden. Last two days have been
fine and it is a relief to begin to get dried out again. Am on call
here at camp today. Washed Henry this a.m., then fed him oil
and grease, getting fully as much on myself as in Henry.

Had a nice day yesterday. The day before was out on one
of the advanced posts. Pretty quiet, only one run. Enjoyed the
day because my bed was in the Captain's office where there
was a good fire. However, when warmed up, the fleas wake up,
so you see being warm has its drawbacks.

Yesterday a.m., as I was leaving with three *poilus* [French
soldiers] for the field hospital, orders came to take two
women away back in the interior. It was a beautiful day and
about a 70-mile trip, so I welcomed it. No breakfast, however,
and no dinner in sight, but at [censored] where I left the *poilus*, I ran over to Doc's, the New York chef. His wife gave me
some bread and butter and a piece of pie. At the next town,
where I dropped a sous-lieutenant, I saw a French cook I
knew and he gave me a small meat pie. Made the trip from
there on in about one and one-half hours, arriving at [cen-
sored] at two o'clock.

It was a fine trip. When I let the women out, the younger
one offered me ten francs or $2.00, but, of course, we are not
in the taxi business. Then the family asked if I would like a
little wine. So I went in and four or five women got dinner.
Finally the food came: Fine soup, four fried eggs, jelly, cheese,

bread, and coffee. That was worth more than ten francs to me. I talked more French than I ever talked in one day before. The French are certainly a hospitable people. Wherever you go, they at least bring out the black bread and wine. They never drink water here, and always laugh when they see any of us doing so.

One day Joe Lee and I walked to the next town for dinner and bath. Had sour-kraut and pork and liked it! Then our friend the Doc and ourselves started for a walk. First we called on his father-in-law. From there we went to see his mother, but she wasn't at home. Then we walked to the next village to see an aunt and many cousins. It was fine, but can you imagine me strolling around this country with an ex-New York chef, weighing 250 lbs, and hobnobbing with his relatives? Certainly do enjoy it, though, and the country is beautiful.

Tomorrow night, Joe and I are going over to the same town to take dinner with the Mayor's family. His son speaks very good English and they are very fine people. So we look forward to a very pleasant evening. Hope the Boches don't start something and spoil it for us.

Love to all, Roger[11]

~

"NEVER TOUCH A FORD AS LONG AS IT RUNS"

March 20, 1918

Dear Family,

Don't know as I have much to say tonight, but as long as I am doing a few letters, will wind up by writing you. Tomorrow I am maid of all work in the kitchen. All I have to do is carry water, chop wood, wash dishes for twenty-five men

three times, serve the food, clean all the cooking pans, and
any other odd jobs the cook may think of. That's fighting for
one's country, all right. I would rather take chances with a
little thing like Fritz's shell fire, than work for a cook. Only
comes once in twenty days, so guess I will live through it.

Had a nice day Sunday up at one of the front posts.
Beautiful day, much spring in the air. Sat out in the back yard
studying French and talking to a *poilu* with a boil on his neck,
watching the French planes patrol the lines, listening to the
lonely shells whirring over-head and going nowhere in particular. In the evening, listened to a *poilu* tell the sad tale of
how he went home on permission and his wife had left. Then
I went to bed and had a good night's rest, after an alcohol rub.
Gee! It felt good!

The next morning, it was so fine that after having my
coffee in bed (as is usual at the Posts, for that is all they get),
I felt so ambitious I decided to blow up a tire. I did, but the
poor old thing, it could not stand the pressure and blew out.
When finally I got away at 10:15, I had blown out two more.
Moral—never touch a Ford as long as it runs.

Today just rain. Read, shivered and smoked this a.m. This
afternoon, about five o'clock I got a couple of chaps to help
me chop wood for tomorrow, I believe in preparedness, you
see. They have led a pretty quiet life here the last few days, but
the lid may blow off any time.

Must close now. I certainly would like to see you all, but I
wouldn't change places today with anyone who is over there.

Don't worry and love to you all.

Roger

P.S. Forgot to say we went to the dinner I spoke of. This
chap that invited us is a French artillery sergeant. He speaks
very good English. His father is Mayor of the city, entertains
Gen. Petain and other notables besides ourselves.

We went over, had tea served by his sister at five o'clock. Then walked until 6:30 and had dinner at seven. Now for the dinner: Soup first of course; then steak and mushrooms. Good? My Lord, yes! Then more steak, then spinach, eggs, and potatoes, then a wonderful meat pie and sponge cake with jelly and real whipped cream. Also four different kinds of light wines. After dinner, coffee was served in the sitting room. Then the two daughters played violin and piano and finally the Mayor himself played the violin. We felt considerably honored. Joe also played a little American rag, and that completed the evening. It was mighty fine for us and we greatly enjoyed, not just the food, but the service, the home, and real people again.

Roger[12]

~

"I HOPE EVERY FOOT OF GROUND AT HOME IS UNDER CULTIVATION"

March 23, 1918

Dear Family,

Another Sunday come and almost gone. It is really surprising how rapidly the time passes, all things considered.

We have been getting the reports today of the big drive against the British; and while they seem terrible, it is only to be expected. It is the greatest thing of the war and let us hope and pray it is the final effort of a misguided people.

It is livening up all along the line, having considerable artillery action here, and much air work. Was evacuating (carrying out the *blessés* or wounded) in the city, about 20 minute drive from here, last night, when they sounded the air-raid signal. Was just taking the last *blessé* out of the car. The doctor asked me if I wanted to stay at the hospital until after the raid. But as they killed several there the night before, I said "no," for I was pining for the open spaces outside the gates.

Another chap was waiting for me at the square, and believe me we left that city in a hurry. Went outside a ways and then stopped the car. They were playing the powerful search lights on the sky and firing the anti-aircraft guns. It was a great sight, but we decided that discretion was much better than valor, just then, and we hit the breeze for home.

There must be a Boche plane overhead here now, for they are firing near here. Excuse me while I step out and see. Just passing over for another raid.

LATER— Easter morning and raining hard. Am afraid it will spoil the Easter parade and it is really too bad, for the countryside has made great preparation for it. One of the most ugly men I have ever seen, who works where we live, has actually shaved and changed his shirt. I am quite sure it is the first time since we arrived here.

I suppose you are writing and watching the reports of the big battle as anxiously as we are. It is too incomprehensible in its greatness for the world at large to understand. We thought for a time we were to stay here, but now it looks as if there is a chance of getting into it. We are all glad not only to get the chance of seeing something of the greatest battle of all times, but also to do something to help.

I hope every foot of ground at home is under cultivation. You should see the way they terrace the hill-sides in this country, just so they can be cultivated. If they only used a little modern equipment along with science, France would be a much richer country. Of course the horses are mostly gone, and you quite often see the last steer and cow yoked up together with a woman leading and an old man holding an antique plow that was undoubtedly the original property of

KEEP *it* COMING

"We must not only
feed our Soldiers
at the front but
the millions of
women & children
behind our lines"

Gen. John J. Pershing

WASTE NOTHING

UNITED STATES FOOD ADMINISTRATION

Those on the US home front were entreated to "waste nothing" and to produce as much food as possible for the war effort. WHI IMAGE ID 64210

his grandfather. One thing that does surprise you, though, is that nearly every small village through here at least, has the electric light plant.

They are closing the mail now, so must close.

Keep well and don't worry.

My love to you all. Roger[13]

⌒

"ONE GOOD BED WITH A FEATHER TICK"

Around April 10, 1918

Dear Family,

Now I am willing to take oath that it is Tuesday. But as to
the date, well, can't say, but it is around the tenth of April. I
am sitting on the ledge of a window of an old château said to
be 500 years old. I can believe it, for it certainly shows signs
of remarkable age.

We arrived here about ten o'clock Sunday night, after
spending five days on the road, traveling and awaiting orders
at different points. The trip was delightful. Saw some wonderful country and it was, by far, the easiest trip we have made.
Always before these jumps have been more like a nightmare,
driving like mad part of the day and night, then sleeping
in cars.

I had a fine French chap with me, a man about forty years
old who was Mayor of his town before the war, and a Baron if
they were to use titles. We would start about 6:30 a.m. before
the rest, in order to reach the destination early and have quarters arranged by the time the convoy arrived. This made it
very pleasant, and I generally prevailed on some kind French
lady to take me in for the night. No matter how the house
may look from both outside and in, there is always one good
bed with a feather tick that they will let you have for a franc
or two.

Yes! I can tell you how many men we have in our section. Just now I think it is 37. We have 20 ambulances, one
small Ford truck, a one-ton Packard, and a Ford touring car,

a motorcycle and a trailer kitchen. We have two cooks, two mechanics, twenty regular drivers, three non-commissioned officers. The rest, well, act as substitute drivers and aids, and when we go up from here to the front, we will need everyone. We are on *repos* here waiting for orders to go up and do our part. We can see the flashes of guns at night and can hear them always.

These are going to be trying times for all of you back home with sons and sweethearts over here. But we'll all just have to put our trust in the Lord and do our part. Don't worry if you do not hear as regularly, for postal service at the front is bad now.

Much love to all, Roger[14]

⤳

"SOMEWHERE IN FRANCE LEADING THE LIFE OF NOMADS"

Sunday, April 22, 1918

Dear Family,

The third Sunday en route and we are still somewhere in France leading the life of nomads. Waiting for orders now, the next move will take us to real work in this great battle that is now going on. Am anxious to be in it, but realize that when once we start, it will mean a long siege of hard, trying work with undoubtedly some casualties coming our way. So we are willing to enjoy this breathing spell. After seven months active work and three weeks on the road, we are all a bit tired. We are now entitled to our first six-months' service stripes, but have not had opportunity to get them yet.

We are camped in a very pretty little town. Our cars are all
lined up in a little wood patch with our kitchen in a farmyard
about ten rods down the road. Some of us are sleeping in the
cars and others in barns. I am of the former.

Will tell you how I have my car arranged. First we have
big sheet iron covers over them and I assure you it has all the
conveniences of a one-room apartment for a family of eight
with a dog. We are still carrying our beds. I have mine placed
in position on one side of the car with various things underneath. Have my blankets all spread out ready for use when
we stop. On front wall have nails, where my hat, helmet, gas
masks, razor straps, etc. hang. On floor next to head of bed, I
have my jewel case; said jewel case being a small wooden box
containing cigarettes and tobacco, writing material, pictures,
etc. Next have a box containing my boots, felt and rubber,
extra shoes, oil-skins, etc. On top of that, is the bag belonging
to the Frenchman who rides with me. Then to fill up, have
two good-sized boxes from the French office. On top of my
bed, when running, I have my barracks bag, containing clothing, etc and suitcase belonging to the Frenchman.

When we stop for the night, I pull out the two French
boxes, place one underneath the car, other in front, place barracks bag and suitcase on front seat, light the lantern, and we
are ready for bed. Then in the morning I draw water out of a
side tank on car for washing.

When we struck this town, had not had a chance to wash
for two days, so was some dirty. I came on first to look up
quarters and while waiting saw a barber shop sign, "shave four
cents, haircut 11 cents." I flattered myself by thinking I needed
a haircut as it was getting a bit long around the edges. Went in
the house and found the barber was a young female. If there

is one thing I am particular about it is this, the cutting of my hair, for just one slip and I might be bald! Decided to take the chance but told her to take it easy. She made about four jabs with the clippers, perhaps as many with the shears, two swipes with a razor and then said "Voilà," meaning that it was finished. When I looked in the glass, I knew she was right, for my hair won't need another cut until the war is over.

This afternoon I am going over to a Canadian Foresters' Camp to see a ball game. We have been fortunate the last few days in passing through English Camps where they have Y.M.C.A. and canteens. Therefore, I've been able to buy a few cigarettes, chocolate, and toothpaste. This new order with the French army will hit us pretty hard, for we are never in touch with Y.M.C.A. or American canteen. We not only don't get the advantages of the American army, but we have only the rations of the French army, and they are some different. As usual, when on the road, we missed the paymaster. Nearly everyone is flat-broke, and I am nearly so, but manage to keep enough to get milk and eggs when we get to these towns.

Yesterday I took a motor apart and cleaned it. Have traveled from one end of this country to another on this ship, without any tire trouble and only cleaned spark plugs once. That is a pretty good record over the roads I have traveled and carrying the load I do.

Just all keep well, raise a large crop of spuds, and don't forget how to bake a few things like mince pies, and cakes. I hope it won't be very long before I will step in and eat you out of house and home. We on this side are not worrying about the final outcome, but there is much fighting and work to be done before it comes.

Much love, Roger[15]

⌁

"THIS KILLING SIMPLY CAN'T
GO ON INDEFINITELY"

May 10, 1918

My Dear Family,

The R.F.D. of France is working pretty well these days, for I received mail from you yesterday and again today. Of course it does not get up to where we are, but the Lieutenant goes back in the interior every few days for some spare parts for cars, and sometimes he is lucky in finding mail along the way.

We have been here about a week now and have been getting our money's worth I assure you. Anything we went through last winter was play compared with this. Today has been pretty quiet. Guess Fritz is taking a day off to bury the dead. The loss of life is, of course, terrible, but he has paid many times over for every foot of ground he has gained. Of course our losses have been heavy too, but nothing in comparison with his. When you see it this close, you wonder more than ever what it is all about and where it is going to end. The end is bound to come, and really don't think it very far off. This killing simply can't go on indefinitely.

We are well located here as far as quarters are concerned. There was a Canadian hospital here at one time, but of course, too close to the lines now. We are sleeping and eating in the unused buildings. If I were to pick out a quiet spot for a vacation, I would not choose this place, however, for there is heavy artillery all around us and a railroad at our back door that Fritz tries for all the time. But it is surprising how accustomed one gets to the bombardment. The *post* where we get most of the *blessés* is a mighty warm spot. One of the boys

This crumbling château was an American Ambulance Field Service Post in World War I. The cellar of the building provided space for operating rooms, dressing rooms, and officers' quarters, housing some fifty men. WHI IMAGE ID 126179

just came in and said it had been hit twice this afternoon, but no one was hurt. There is a crossroads about five or ten rods from the post that Fritz tries for most of the time. When a car comes up to the post or goes down, we always watch to see it come around the corner and then cheer. Believe me, we don't hesitate any coming around that corner. Some mighty close calls, but so far, no casualties.

Most of the work is at night and it is a tough job to drive over these terrible roads without lights, pitch dark, and with the munition convoys and trucks going and coming. Generally lose a radiator every night. When anything hits a Ford, it is good-bye Ford!

We go on a short *repos* tomorrow or next day—a good thing, for everyone is about sick with colds, dust, and work. I have been laid up for two days, but am feeling better tonight.

Love to all, Roger[16]

⌒

"DODGING A SHELL HOLE HERE,
AND A DEAD HORSE THERE"

May 24, 1918

My Dear Family,

Am beginning to feel rested again, and it's a good feeling
for I was sure tired. Ten and one-half months in the army, and
eight months on the front is quite a stretch. And believe me,
the last ten days was the climax. After we came down here
from the lines, it seemed to me as if the war must be over, and
that we were ready to go home. But I was wrong. Now they
have assigned us to another division and we'll go back again
shortly. They say we are a good section and I guess that is the
reason, for there are sections here that have not seen action
yet. Well, guess we can stand it.

Don't know what I told you of our last work, for felt so
rotten, and was so tired, that my mind was registering zero.
We had a right lively time of it, and caught it as hard as we
could without being on a retreating front. I probably mentioned that we were camped in the center of some heavy artillery, with a cemetery in front of us and a railroad just back
of us. It was a warm spot, for Fritz seemed to be trying for all
three, and he is a fair shot.

The last few nights we were there, he came over in his
bombing planes, and that is bad business. One car on duty
at hospital about 300 yards from us was blown to little bits.
Luckily the driver was not in it. That was the only car we lost.
As for radiators, lights, and fenders—well, it was a quiet night
if we did not lose several. It is a strange feeling that one has
going down a shelled road, with them bursting all around,

dodging a shell hole here, and a dead horse there, rounding the last corner where Fritz drops shells regularly, without throwing a tire, and running over spilled hand grenades.

Yes, it is a great feeling to make that last corner, then turn into the *Post de Secour*, back your car around and run for the sand bags. When you get there you light a cigarette, heave a sigh of thankfulness and say to yourself, "If I ever get back to Clinton and Dewey, where only Billy Wilkinson disturbs the peace twice a day, just let me stay."

As I said, our rest is about over and we'll get more of the same. We don't mind the work and we can stand the sights. I suppose Fritz will be starting his supreme effort in a few weeks, as this is the kind of weather he likes. I saw some Boche prisoners one morning being taken down. They came right thru our camp, and they were fairly jumping with joy to be out of it. But he is not beaten by a long ways, and I'm glad that some in the U.S. are waking up to the fact. It is worth any cost and sacrifice to keep this struggle away from our own dooryard. Any man or woman who is lukewarm over winning this war, would need only to see an old couple walking up a shelled road to get something they had forgotten in their home, and then to find their home gone!

You asked about our meals. We are allowed seventy cents a day from our government for food. But as we are attached to the French Army, we can only buy fifty cents worth a day per man from them. We get our meat, potatoes, beans, rice, bread, sugar, etc from them. Then with the extra money we buy extras from the stores. Lately I have been buying eggs at 85 cents a dozen, a little butter at 90 cents a lb, salad, cauliflower, cheese, etc. We have to buy all our breakfasts extra, as the French breakfast is coffee and bread. When I get to the British canteen, I buy shredded wheat

biscuits and oatmeal. It's really not bad, but on the front it's
hard to get a variety. If the Frenchman has his bread and red
wine, he'll get along, but that does not satisfy us. We miss
good water most of all.

Had mail yesterday from you. "Ain't it a grand and glorious feeling" to get mail.

Much love, Roger[17]

◦ᴗ

"HOME AGAIN WHERE THE SHELLS
ARE WHISTLING OVERHEAD"

June 4, 1918

My Dear Family,

Well, after two weeks *repos* we are home again where
the shells are whistling overhead, and where we get plenty
of exercise for our back, by dodging down as we hear them
coming. It's funny how when you hear that whistle, you natu-
rally flatten out. We are digging ourselves an *abri* (shelter) in
case they really shell us. As usual, there is artillery all around
us, and we are camped on an evacuated farm with many
trees. The trees are fine for camouflage, but Fritz generally
figures that where there are trees, there are men, and he acts
accordingly.

We are a tent colony this time, having borrowed tents
from the English. I am in a nice camouflaged one, so like
the ostrich, feel very safe—not. The weather is still good,
although for the last few days it has been threatening. I dug a
trench around our tent last night and when it rains will know
just how rotten an engineer I am.

Well, he started the big push again and that misguided son of the "Old Un" seems to have had good initial success. We heard once they were within twenty miles of Paris. We were about ready to pack up and leave, but was contradicted of course, later. Now what little news we get is encouraging, and we all have great faith in General Foch. The Americans are taking their part shoulder to shoulder with the others and doing fine from what we hear. The *poilu* is tickled to death over it too. I think Fritz has a great big healthy respect for our boys, for not once has he been able to gain and hold anything against them. When this is all history, I feel sure that our "Dough Boy" will rank along with the Australians and Canadians as fighters of the fighting type.

Am feeling fine and am picking up some lost weight, but not enough to worry about. I sure couldn't get a job as a fat man in a side show. Was out yesterday after feed. This buying food certainly has aided me in learning to speak French, for with what French I know and my hands, I get along pretty well. When I get home, probably would have hard work talking, if my hands were tied. The British canteens help. I really depend on them for extras and of course their prices are much better than the civil stores. Makes me quite homesick to walk into one and see shelves lined with American goods.

We won't have nearly the work here, probably, that we had on the other sector, but Fritz does much more shelling here. He did not have the chance before, for we were doing it. I haven't been up to the front post yet, but they say it is a fright, and the last 300 yards of road nearly impassable. First day a shell hit beside one of the cars. The concussion blew the sides inward and the top off, pulling out the nail that held

the canvas down. We'll probably be here the better part of a
month, but don't know of course.

These are serious times and anxious ones for all. I believe
you at home have the hardest part to bear, I mean mothers,
fathers, etc. But keep a stiff upper lip, and don't ever let your
"wind get up" as they say over here. According to last figures,
we have lost many more men from sickness than from the
war. Guess the mortality rate of those in the States is higher
than ours over here. This Mutual Cheering Society that we
have is fine. I try to cheer you up a bit; and then when your
letters come, they do the same for me. Hope I get ten today.

Will close now and get another blister swinging a pick.
Love to all. Roger[18]

◦

" 'TIS A WONDERFUL SIGHT, BUT THE
RESULTS ARE NOT PRETTY"

June 10, 1918

My Dear Family,

Have moved twice since last letter, but still working the
same sector. Fritz is very systematic in everything he does
you know. The place where we were had not been shelled any,
so one afternoon while I was out buying food, he opened up
and gave the boys a chance to try the trench. We expected
it again at night, and sure enough we hit the trench three
times. We would stand there with our helmets just sticking
out, and when we would hear the terrible whistle of the shell,
everyone would duck down. Lord, my legs were stiff the next
morning! The last time we were in, one of the boys on duty
came in with three *blessés*. His car had been hit when about
two hundred yards from camp and his men all wounded

again. The Lieutenant bound up their wounds with my assistance. I guess I will need a new overcoat next winter.

We are camping now in a nice green pasture with a row of trees all around. Plenty of noise, but no shells in camp up to present. With the boys working all night, you must have the camp in a place where they can sleep when off duty. Our work is not as heavy as when we were up before, for there is little infantry action. Then we were straightening out the lines, and attacking nearly every night. It is a wonderful sight at night to see a barrage start, before an attack. Everything will be very quiet, so much so that it's almost suspicious. Then, all of a sudden, you will see the flashes, and hundreds of guns will fire at once. The flashes are like fire flies over a swamp, and the roar of the guns like thousands of big drums going at the same time. Then the signals for artillery, they are beautiful.

Yes—'tis a wonderful sight, but the results are not pretty. All the small villages here are deserted and practically demolished. It is a weird feeling, driving through a fair-sized town at night, deserted except for the police on the corners—just the ghostly walls left of the buildings. The churches in the towns or villages near the front have almost all been hit. Some have walls only that are standing, while others just have huge holes in the roofs or side walls. Surely Fritz must pay for this.

Yes, you must have enjoyed the sight of the boys from Camp Grant and I thank the Lord that that is all you will see of this war. The real thing is somewhat different, but it is a wonderful and inspiring sight nevertheless.

Well this is a considerable letter. Our mail doesn't get away very often so don't worry when you don't hear regularly.

Remember me kindly to the family and friends and much love to you all.

Roger[19]

⌁

"A REAL AMERICAN LADY CAME OUT
WITH HOT COFFEE"

July 13, 1918

My Dear Family,

Back in sunny France once more. I am sure of the France
part at least, but the sunny part is only tradition, judging from
the sample we have had thus far.

We were in Belgium as you probably guessed. We left the
front on the 6th and embarked on train the 9th. When we
found we were to go by train, it didn't make much of a hit
with us; but as the Lieutenant said, it would be a new experience. It was. The next train I ride on, I hope will be either the
Pennsylvania or New York Central, taking me back to Chicago. As we have twenty-five cars or *voitures* as the French say,
we had twenty-five flat cars, one freight car for sleeping 37
men, and one first class car for officers. We left Tuesday afternoon at five o'clock and unloaded Thursday morning at 9:13.
We passed within sight of Paris, but did not have the good
luck to stop off. Had bought a lot of canned goods, enough
for four days, so lived on canned ham, beef, sardines, etc, trying to have coffee twice a day. As we drew near to Paris, the
Red Cross generally had hot coffees at all the cities where the
train stopped.

The morning we pulled into the city where we unloaded, a
real American lady came out with hot coffee. She was the first
woman who really spoke our own language, dressed in familiar clothes, without wooden shoes, that we had seen in some
eight months. Can you imagine just how good she looked to
us? I doubt whether you can.

After unloading and having a bit to eat, we drove about twenty-five miles. We are now camping along a river, fighting mosquitoes, eating canned goods and moldy bread, and expecting to go in the line again any day. Believe me the life of R.A. Skinner (in charge of mess) these days isn't worth much. I am thankful I start out buying fresh food again tomorrow— you know I never did care much for sardines.

Love, Roger[20]

~

"THE BIG PUSH WAS ON AND THE FORDS WERE NECESSARY"

July 18, 1918

Dear Family,

A lull in the battle on our sector today. So have been straightening up the camp, making up mess accounts, and now will write letters. Will try to give you the details of the last few days in order, and then you will have a better idea of events in general.

I think that my last letter was written from our first camp after getting off the train. We were there three nights (almost), for at three a.m. orders came in to move the camp about ten miles further up. This was the morning of the 14th or the French 4th of July. We had had a hard trip down and were tired physically and tired of "canned horse" and believe me we growled when we had to pull out so early.

Pulled into the next town about 5:30 and parked the cars over a champagne cellar containing millions of bottles. I was busy all morning getting the kitchen in shape, but caught a short nap in the afternoon.

I slept that night in a small house built onto the large
house where we had our kitchen located. I asked the lady
to give me a room with a bed, but she could not, and it was
mighty lucky for me that she had none. About 1:30 a.m. the
Boche started shelling the back areas, as is usual with this
hellish way of making war. The first thing I realized was a
terrible explosion, then screams and then boards and bricks
lying all over the courtyard. The brick dust was so thick it
was impossible to see five feet ahead of you. The main part of
the house was hit with a large shell, killing the little girl (ten
years old) and badly wounding her mother. The two other
boys and myself, who were sleeping perhaps twenty feet away,
were uninjured. That was the only direct hit in the village. We
went into a dugout for a time, then back to bed, but this time
lying on the ground by the cars. It seems as if God must soon
punish these fiends who make war on women and children.

Orders came in again at three a.m. to move on up. Although the division had not gone in the lines, the Big Push
was on and the Fords were necessary. We started about four
a.m. and came up a
road where Fritz was
laying shells down
one after another.
The car I was in was
hit with shrapnel,
but we all arrived
at camp. The Lieu-
tenant and one of
the Sergeants went
directly to our Colo-
nel for orders. By the
time we had the cars
unloaded, the call for

American ambulances are lined up and
ready for the convoy to begin, ca. 1919.
WHI IMAGE ID 126146

cars came in from a nearby field hospital. By 7:30 a.m. every car was out helping other sections. About 9:30 word came down from the post that one of our men, who had just been sent out, had been killed.

I tell you it struck us pretty hard. We had been mighty fortunate, not having any killed before in eight months continuous service on the front. At Mt Kemmel we had one gassed and at the Loere one slightly wounded by shrapnel.

Well, all cars were out for twenty-four hours and some for thirty. Never saw such a steady stream of wounded, and our losses were nothing as compared with the Boche. It took us from two to three hours to unload the cars after we reached the hospital.

Late that evening of the first day, the Lieutenant came back. He couldn't locate five of the cars that had gone out to assist another section. He was about all in, so I said I would go. Took another chap with me, and we finally found the post by following an ambulance. In getting there, we ran past trenches filled with *poilus* ready for fighting. We sure thought we were getting pretty close to the lines. When we got to this place, we found some of the men, but some had gone up still farther to evacuate a post in a town the Boche had taken one side of. So you see just how close we go when necessary.

Coming back got lost a couple of times for the roads that are the safest are simply tracks through the fields. It is a Chinese puzzle to locate the right one. Finally found one I wanted—it was marked by a dead horse, so arrived in camp OK.

There was little infantry action on our sector the next day, but of course the guns kept up a steady roar. I left about eight o'clock with the Lieutenant to visit all the posts, pull in the men loaned to other sections, see our *Chef* for further orders, etc. That kept us going all day. Then about ten o'clock we

started out to see the Colonel or *Chef* again. He told us to pull
in two more cars, so we went after them. In going after the
second car, we took a short road where we had to pass over a
bridge. Coming back, the Lieutenant went ahead in his car,
and I came in the last car. The chap driving didn't know the
way and the dust was so thick one could not follow closely.
We lost the Lieutenant at once, and when we came to the
road which crossed the bridge, a guard stopped us saying we
should go on around the next village. I told him we had just
come by the bridge road; then he said it would be impossible
to return that way for the bridge had been hit and blown up.
Of course we thought the Lieutenant had gone that way and
had been caught, but when we arrived in camp there he was
wondering "where in hell" we had been.

Yesterday everyone in camp rested up in the a.m.—ter-
ribly hot. In the afternoon, we went over to the cemetery
where our boy was buried and had the funeral service. A
French priest officiated. There were also a number of French
artillerymen there burying their dead. After our funeral we all
passed in review, Americans and French, and then we did the
same with them.

Talked with a French aviator observer, day before yesterday, who had been forced to land. He said the German
trenches were completely filled with the dead. Please don't
worry too much, for by the time this reaches you, this particular affair will undoubtedly be over. The worry and uncertainty
are for you. With us, it is one day or one hour after another. If
the Big Moment does come for us over here, it is the biggest
thing we can do, and it is to every mother, father, wife, sister,
or sweetheart not to mourn, but to be proud of the one who
has had the chance to do, not perhaps great things, but simply
what he could.

I want to see you all, as you know; I want to loaf around the parks, etc; I want many things "over there," but I wouldn't trade places with anyone on that side of the water today.

Love, Roger[21]

~

"THE GRAND PIANO LOOKED LIKE
A TOY MUSIC BOX"

August 24, 1918

My Dear Family,

Well, here I am back at the front again after my seven days leave and glad to be here. I could have stood another week there at Chambery, but I feel 100 percent better for the few days I did have. Was very much disgusted with it all the first day; but when my nerves let down, and I began to get rested, I really enjoyed it. Nothing wildly exciting, but just a good rest.

I had several fine auto trips with the secretary, Miss Davidson; otherwise, probably would not have seen much of the country. The mountains and lakes were beautiful, and such a relief from the country where we are now. Reminded me a great deal of California, except that the mountain sides are all cultivated. The thing that surprised me most, though, was the behavior of the boys up there. I did not see a case of drunkenness all the time I was there. The girls that worked there said it was always the same. Guess just the sight of the American girls around was enough to make them keep their self-respect. The first evening I was there they had a dance. I had quite made up my mind that I was too old to dance. But when one of the hostesses came up with two charming girls, I fell of course. Later, found one has two brothers who belong to my fraternity, and the other girl had lived in Chicago, and knew some people I knew. So I greatly enjoyed the evening.

The next day these two girls, who were on their leave also, John Wood, a boy from our section, and I walked out to Rousseau's old château. Very interesting, but I think I prefer modern conveniences. There was such a crowd there, they shipped us out a day early. We left at five o'clock and after standing for ten solid hours, we arrived at Dijon. So crowded that we could not even move our feet. As we had an extra day, we left the train there, for I ached so I was nearly crazy. Walked across town to the American Red Cross canteen, where the two girls we had met at Chambery were on duty. One of them was on service there at four a.m. and she gave us blankets and floor space after feeding us, so we had a couple of hours sleep. We intended going on in the morning, but when we got up, we found a note asking us to stay over for lunch.

About 9:30 the girls came down after us. We shopped a bit, then went up to the old 18th century château where they

The men are all smiles at an American Red Cross canteen in France. WHI
IMAGE ID 132558

were living with a Duchess—a wonderful place. John Wood
went off on another shopping tour, but knowing Miss W. had
a very fine voice, I asked her to sing for me. She took me into
the large drawing room where the grand piano looked like a
toy music box and sang to me for an hour. I had not realized
how starved I was for good music. Afterwards we had a real
American lunch. They fed us so much that I thought we never
would be able to move again. John and a Miss Grant, who
went to Beloit College, went out with the Duke in his car, so I
took a blanket and went down by the little lake and had a nap
while the other two girls were on duty at the canteen. I woke
up about five and then one of the girls took me in to see the
Duchess and tour the château. We took dinner at the canteen
with the girls and then waited for our train. It was a wonderful day and evening. Caught a three a.m. train for Paris, and
had to stand all the way.

Back in the lines now, but on a very quiet front, as quiet as
Brodhead on a Sunday morning. However, we probably will
not be here long, and can stand it as have had considerable
excitement the past few months.

When I was on leave I saw some colored troops. Was
talking with one of them one day and he said: "I like fightin',
but I tell you I always gives them poor Huns a chance." I said,
"You do, how's that?" "Well, when I meet one of them there
Huns out in No-Man's-Land, I says to him, you either jump
on this here bayonet, or I'll run it through you." Some choice
I say.

Well General Foch is certainly keeping the Boche on the
move now, and he is showing the German High Command
up. Do you realize that a wonderful piece of work it was to
stop the last Boche offensive in two days, and then start the
counter drive? The Americans and French did wonderful
work, and then the moment the lines were straightened out,

the English and French start again. If they keep this up for the
rest of the fall, I think Fritz will have had enough. I am ready
to come home any time now.

Love to all, Roger[22]

~

"THE BEGINNING OF THE END
IS SURELY AT HAND"

October 12, 1918

My Dear Ones,

Just a few lines tonight as I may run into town tomorrow
and perhaps get a chance to mail this.

We are following up the big push, and just at present are
having a difficult time keeping up with Fritz. The first few
days, perhaps a week, we had work and work only. Weather
has been rotten; rainy and cold all the time, but I manage to
feel mighty well. Ours is the only section of this army that has
followed up with the troops. By that I mean camp, etc. We
stored our baggage and are traveling light. Have been sleeping
under trees, under the sky, in old Boche trenches, in fact any
place and time we get a chance. I think I have a cross between
U.S., French, and Boche cooties; and they sure are giving me
hell. Gee, I certainly will be glad when I can get into decent
linen and "cits" again and sleep a night through without
scratching. What makes me sore is I have never seen one of
the darn things.

Having more rain tonight. When we hit camp late night
before last, I slept with one of the boys underneath his pup-
tent. We nearly broke our backs getting in and out, so decided
to dig in the next morning. We dug down about three feet
wide and long enough for two flops, put our tents over the

hold and now very "comfy." Only a few yards away is a Boche trench where three Fritzies still lie, who did not get away.

Sights of the war are a bit horrible, but a very common sight for us these days. We have been in for sixteen days now and are fed up with it, but we'll surely last it out. The beginning of the end is surely at hand; and I sincerely believe, God permitting, we'll all be coming home soon.

Eight letters today. The first good mail in months.

October 19, 1918

First day of *repos* after being in the lines since the 25th of September. Have written several letters, but none of them have been sent. Am going into ⌊censored⌋ where you received the postal card from, to buy food and am going to cable from there if I can.

It has been a great experience, but it has also been a taste of hell, following up an advancing army with the terrible weather, sleeping any time and any place. Have felt remarkably well through it all. This is a punk letter, but it's just to let you know I am O.K. and that I am thinking of you.

Much love to all.

Your son, Roger[23]

❦

"OH, THE SIGHTS OF WAR!"

October 22, 1918

My Dear Family:

This is the first real chance I have had to write any of you since September 25th. Have sent a couple of short notes, but cabled a few days ago and hope it reached you before you did too much worrying.

Don't know whether I can give you a good description
of the past weeks or not, but will do my best. We heard
days ahead there was to be an attack here, but only rumors
of course. I went into town the 25th; and when I got back
to camp late, I found them all packed and ready to leave. I
grabbed a box containing my smokes, etc, stuck it in an ambulance, and away we went.

It took us about three hours to go six miles, the roads were
so crowded. We pulled into our new camp just as the barrage
started. It was a beauty; just a steady roll of thunder and the
whole sky was one great flash. It sure gave the Boche hell,
as we could see when we started to follow up. We remained
at this camp two days with not much work to do. Then our
division went in and we moved up. This time we stopped in a
village just behind the old French 1st lines. We were camped
in a field which soon became a sea of mud for it rained all
the time.

We worked night and day for about a week. The night of
my birthday I spent standing on a crossroad corner in pour-
ing rain, directing cars to the posts. The *Post de Secours* kept
changing as our troops advanced. As the trip to the hospital
was very long, the posts were generally changed before the
driver would get back for his next trip.

The second or third day at that place I went with the Lieutenant to visit the posts. The Boche were shelling the road
for practically the first time, as they had had to pull all their
artillery back. We ran on past the first post and were finally
stopped by a string of trucks, cars, and munition wagons.
Fritz had made a direct hit on a big ammunition truck farther
ahead, and the whole road was blocked, while the shells were
popping off like a bunch of fire crackers and going in every
direction. Everyone had left their cars and were in old Boche

Roads are jammed with reserves and supplies behind the Yankee line of advance into St. Mihiel, 1918. WHI IMAGE ID 132647

trenches along the road. It was quite exciting. When they came too close to us, we ran across the road to a *dép abri*, but just as we arrived there with a bunch of *poilus*, one shell burst very close and you should have seen the whole bunch of us run back like a bunch of sheep.

We finally decided we had had enough, and we decided to take a chance on getting back up the road. Believe me, that Ford was turned around in double quick time, and we made it out all right. Fritz did a lot of shelling that afternoon, but his marksmanship wasn't much. However, he made three direct hits on the road.

That same afternoon, while I was standing by one of our *post de secours*, an American colored soldier came along. He was wounded in the hand. I asked him if he was hungry and judge he was for he ate a can of sardines we gave him in about one gulp and almost swallowed the can. Several times a shell would break near and he would say "guess I'll drag on" but we kept telling him to wait and we would give him a ride. Finally one landed pretty close and Mr. Colored Man started down the road saying: "Well, I'm draggin; can't see no use in finishin' gettin' killed here." The same old coon and you should see them grin when they go by with some Boche.

A couple of days later, we moved up again and this time into Boche territory. We had just finished making camp, and were ready for bed when orders came to move again. Well, the atmosphere was rather blue, but we got off without much trouble as we were traveling light. It was dark, and we could not find a field to camp in, so just slept in the road. Lord, it was cold, but we slept.

The next morning we went down the road a ways and found a pretty decent place. I put my pup-tent over a Boche trench. It was very comfortable, but with a crossbreed of English, French, U.S., and Boche cooties working on me nights, I almost went crazy with scratching. We worked from this point for about a week and then moved on up. This time to a village where the Boche had "dug in" in their fashion. It was very interesting. There had been very severe fighting there. The first night we slept in a little hole we had dug within a few yards of Boche machine-gun trenches where the Boche and French were still lying.

Oh, the sights of war! But one thinks nothing of it—just all in a day's work.

It kept raining all the time and the roads were terrible. I was acting top sergeant much of the time up there, so I didn't

see much of the posts. Was kept busy in camp, seeing that
the cars were sent out. We were the only section in the sector
that followed up the advance, and we were the last relieved.
Believe me by October 18th we had had enough. We were
relieved the 19th and started down, but with troops going and
coming we could find no place to stop, so after much talking
with the colonel, he allowed us to come back to our old camp.

Oh, man; it was almost like coming home. The next
two days I spent on the road buying food. Managed to stay
overnight in town and how I did enjoy that bed. Hit the hay
at seven p.m. and it was great. Hadn't had clothes off in over
three weeks, not even shoes. The next morning we started
early to the U.S. commissary, got a good bunch of supplies
and got back about noon. The hotels were all crowded so
bought $2.00 worth of mutton chops and took them to a
little store, where I had bought a good deal of stuff, and they
cooked them for us. We hardly left the bones; it was the first
meal we had had in about four days. Felt remarkably well
through it all and it was a wonderful experience.

Plenty of souvenirs, but you know how much of a hand I
am at collecting souvenirs. Guess I'll be one myself, if I ever
get home and that will satisfy my friends. I'll be glad when
this is all over and can get back to you all again. The end is
near at hand. The Hun is getting a good beating now and is
going to get a worse one before we are through with him.
See lots of U.S. troops now, but have never run across anyone
I know.

Sunday, November 3, 1918

About this time you are getting ready to leave for church and
I can't imagine a more peaceful scene than that in Brodhead
on a Sunday morning. It is some peaceful with us also this
morning. It is in the air, on our tongues, and certainly in our

thoughts. With the latest developments, it would not surprise me if it came at any hour or any day.

As a side light, a small bunch of Boche prisoners just walked by, and one of our Frenchmen called to them in German, "the war is over" and you should have seen them smile.

Last summer when victory looked a long ways off, I did not think so much about the end, but now that it is close, we all want it very, very much. When it really does come, what our feelings will be is hard to say. The hardest part then will be waiting to get back. Of course we in the ambulance service are hoping to be sent back early, for we were among the first 30,000 over here, and we are attached to the French. But it will probably be the other way, and we'll be the last to leave.

Will close now as the crowd is getting too noisy for mental concentration.

Much love to you all. Roger[24]

~

"LA GUERRE EST FINI"

November 12, 1918

My Dear Family,

Alors mes petite enfants, la guerre est fini, n'est ce pas? That is what we have been saying for the last two days—the war is over. Of course this is only an Armistice. But with the conditions imposed, Germany is all through, down and out, and a second-rate power. Her War Lord (?) in flight, the Crown Prince in tears, and the country in a revolution. How is that for a change?

You can imagine how happy and pleased we are, but the thing has come so gradually for us. We have felt so sure that the end was not far off. It was not as great a surprise to us as it was to you all. Also I imagine that you, the ones back home, are the ones most relieved.

We have been on our way down from the lines now for over a week, and are now located in a small village near Chalons. Three of us have a very delightful room with a fireplace. The old lady who owns the house brings us hot chocolate and toast while in bed in the morning. She woke us up yesterday to give us the news.

Later I went to Chalons. Every face had a smile, and everywhere there were French, American, and British flags. If it means a great deal to us, what must it mean to the French.

We had expected to go on yesterday, but of course everything is changed now. We will probably be a part of the Army of Occupation. The rumor is now that we are going to Alsace. As long as we don't come home, I had just as soon go there as any other place. It was just a year ago tomorrow that we arrived on the front here. We have had one busy year. A year that I would not care to live over again, but a year that I would not change for any other year of my life thus far.

Well, I won't be home for Thanksgiving or Christmas, but if the flu don't get me, I ought to be with you by the Fourth of July.

Much love to you all, Roger[25]

~

"WHILE THE SILK HATS ARE SETTLING THE DESTINIES OF THE BOCHE"

November 24, 1918

Dear Family,

Well, we are still hovering around the open fire, enjoying all the comforts that our 21 francs a week affords us. Am

afraid this is the last days of it, however, for it is practically
certain that we shall move tomorrow.

We have been having wonderful weather the last two
weeks—clear and cold days and even colder and clearer
nights. Now that we are to hit the trail again, it is snowing and
raining. What luck, and we can't say: "*c'est la guerre*" any longer. Just between you and me, this peacetime moving doesn't
bring any joy to my life. Am sure the coming months will really be harder for us than any other time has been.

We will probably pass through our old and first stomping
ground, as we are going to Alsace, with the first big stage of
our journey ending at Belfast. It will mean ten days or two
weeks on the road. As long as we have to go somewhere,
while the Silk Hats are settling the destinies of the Boche, I
had just as soon go to Alsace, especially if we pass through
Massevaux and see some of our old friends.

But believe me, *mes parents*, this gypsy life doesn't appeal to
me during the winter months with a climate such as I know ex-
ists where we are going. I still have vivid recollections of push-
ing Fords through two feet of snow, cranking them at three
a.m. with the thermometer twenty below and with a rheumatic
back. We will probably have the same two feet of snow, the
same freezing temperatures, and undoubtedly the same back.

Last winter we were working and learning with expectations for the coming, but now all we have to think about is
when they are going to send us home. We'll probably see a lot
of historical things of interest, but I would much rather see
that line of sky scrapers along Michigan boulevard than any
work of art left standing over here. As for ruins, I think the
sight of the Union Station at four p.m. would fill the bill.

As usual, we start the journey a month behind in pay, but
guess we'll get along. This is a nice, cheerful letter isn't it; and

as long as I feel in this mood, I had better stop. I wrote pretty cheerful letters for sixteen months so you'll forgive me, won't you, if I grouch from now on?

Much love, Roger[26]

⌇

"AT PRESENT WE ARE DOING A JITNEY SERVICE"

December 7, 1918

Dear Family,

Well, Saturday night is here again and I wonder where the week has gone. When I sit down and study the map, it is easy to see we've been covering ground, and we still have considerable more to cover. We are still leading an aimless existence, following our division here and there, wherever there is road space for them. We send cars out to follow each regiment or unit when on march; and many of the officers want cars, so at present we are doing a jitney service.

You will please pardon this scrawl, for I am sitting almost on the back of my neck, so as to get some light on the paper and still keep my feet in the oven. The old lady has just been in to make up the bed, and it looks so high that I am almost afraid to get into it. However I know just how comfortable it will be, for no matter how poor the house may look from the outside, you always find a good bed. Just had a big bowl full of milk; so, all in all, I am quite "comfy."

One thing I have decided is that it does not pay to take baths in the winter time. When I came out of the lines, I started to take baths and kept changing clothing, hoping to rid myself of the cooties. But the cleaner I became, the more the cooties liked me, and I have given up in despair. I guess I

will just have to scratch and have a mighty cootie army until I
get into decent clothes again.

The Lieutenant is still away, but I rather expect him back
tomorrow. Meanwhile, I have been having my hands full with
the French. Was called up to the Chief of Staff's office the
other night. Luckily one of the aids spoke very good English,
so we got along nicely. If I had had to talk French or through
our French interpreter, I couldn't have said the things I did
say. I could explain our position very well in English. They
are demanding so many cars for transporting officers, which
is against the rules, that it leaves us without enough cars to
move our camp.

It is only 8:30, but I am tired tonight, so will hit this pile
of feathers. I want to come home.

Love to all, Roger[27]

⌒

The same early January issue of the *Independent Register* that
contained the last two letters also contained a note about Skinner
in the column entitled "The Boys with the Colors." It read, in
part, as follows:

"CITED FOR BRAVERY"

Mr. Roger Skinner, whose letters from France have been so
heartily enjoyed by hundreds of our readers, has recently
been cited for bravery and is eligible for the French Cross
decoration, as soon as our government takes action to permit
such honors. Roger has been in service more than a year and
was among the first Americans in hospital service to land in
France.[28]

⌒

"THE WONDERFUL AND GLORIOUS
ARMY OF OCCUPATION"

January 25, 1919

My Dear Ones,

We are now a part of the wonderful and glorious Army of Occupation. We left Chalons the latter part of November and after trekking nearly all over France, our division is now holding down a sector on the Rhine east of Colmar. As usual we are quartered in the smallest of villages.

If there is any glory, sport, or whatever you may call it in this business, it is certainly not for us, following up the tail end. One real satisfaction I get out of it though, is to see the

This ambulance is stuck in the mud on the road to the Rhine, December 8, 1918. WHI IMAGE ID 132718

French men quartered in the same house try to talk to the women. All they can say is *"oui, oui"* and not understanding a word. It is a sweet revenge for us who *"oui, oui*-ed" to them for several months. The people seem anxious to please when they find out we aren't barbarians, and I guess the French and Americans are a relief after four years of Germans.

I like Alsace very much and wish I could see it in the summer. The Alsatians are very progressive and we find some who speak English and French. But generally speaking, it is only the very old and the children who speak any French; the in-between generations speak German. When we run into someone who speaks French, it is like running into a Frenchman who spoke English, when we first came over. I remarked to the Lieutenant one day that I thought the French were poor linguists. He said the Americans are the worst, but without being able to speak a word they could generally get what they wanted. That is true, the latter part anyway, because I have seen boys start out, when we would arrive at a town, who could not speak a word of French and yet they would come back in a short time with what they started after and also give the history of the town and its people.

I seem to be getting along pretty well with my German— can't speak a word but by sign language and giving a can of tobacco and a couple of cakes of soap I generally find a bowl of milk in my room after supper. Last night the female of the house gave me some fresh butter and it certainly was delicious. I am feeling better as I am finally rid of my cold which hung on ever since the Argonne.

Colmar is a fine city. Good stores with plenty of everything in the food line, but prices seem high. Cigars are on sale, the first I have seen in months—30 cents for a ten-cent cigar. A bit stiff but welcomed for the change. A good dinner for two at a café costs about thirty francs, $6.00. You go into a tea shop and have 3 or 4 cakes and a cup of chocolate and it costs $1.00.

LATER— I think that our winter has arrived at last and at a very inopportune time; for in two days we expect to start back into France again, probably for Darney, thirty kilometers west of Epinal. We have to cut across the Vosges Mountains at a mighty bad pass, and we may be sent around by Belfast in order to avoid it. I have my doubts as to our cars pulling the steep grades with snow and ice.

At Epinal there is a large French demobilization center; we hope we won't be attached very long after reaching there. We think there is a chance of leaving in March, but it is just a think. I would start walking to port tonight if I could get home.

Hope you are all well and that I will see you soon.

Much love, Roger[29]

~

No further letters from Roger Skinner were printed in either Brodhead newspaper. A note on April 9, 1919, mentioned that he had safely arrived on the East Coast from his voyage across the Atlantic.[30]

By April 23, 1919, Roger Skinner had finally returned home. The *Independent Register* reported the following that day:

"BRODHEAD IS PROUD OF THIS SOLDIER'S RECORD"

Mr. & Mrs. W.R. Skinner and Master Albert Broughton went to Janesville on Thursday evening to meet Sergeant Roger Skinner, who received his discharge at Camp Grant last week. He is now at the home of his parents for a few weeks' rest, and he surely shows the need of it. He left France just exactly

nineteen months from the day he landed there during all of
which time he was in a French ambulance service or acting
with a supply division. He served on two entire expeditions
from the Swiss border to the extreme northern end of the
French lines and was in the ambulance and hospital service
following many of the severest battles of the war, and during
this wide experience probably had a better opportunity to see
the horrors of the conflict than befell to most our boys.

Like most men who saw much of the actual conflict and
the sorrows of modern warfare, Roger is reticent in relating
what he actually saw, and with becoming modesty has little
to say of his own exploits. We do know, however, that the
French comrades with whom he served must have formed
an attachment, for Roger speaks in most complimentary
manner of his association with the men of the French armies
with whom he came in contact and with some of whom he
spent several months. In all the nineteen months, he saw but
two persons whom he had ever met before in this country
and one can sense that he must have felt that he was serving
another country during these months, yet we know that in
all the conflict he was serving America, whose interests were
so closely linked with France that the war was considered a
war for all of civilization. It may be explained that when Mr
Skinner entered the service, the American ambulance service had not been developed, and being anxious to get into
useful action, he was attached to a French division and it was
never deemed necessary thereafter to separate him from his
French comrades.

He brought home many attractive souvenirs of the
battlefield, including a German revolver which grips the
admiration of every admirer of firearms, a Spanish revolver
used by the French, a gas mask, a helmet, boots, photos, two
handsome brass vases made from the shells of the famous

French 75 gun, the gun which the French say won the war, and last but not least, his own decoration, a French *Croix de Guerre*, presented to him because of some particularly brave soldierly service, which Roger doesn't tell about because of his tantalizing modesty.

He returned on the U.S. Ship *Grant*, and suffered an attack of the flu on the way over, which pulled him down about twenty pounds, which twenty pounds he will likely regain under his parental roof before he returns to work.

Brodhead is proud of this soldier's record in the conflict, particularly proud because we had never thought of Roger as anything but a soldier of good fortune, one used to the comforts of civilian life, and unfitted apparently to the rugged requirements of the battlefield. Under stress of the world's need, the stuff that was in him, was developed.

It's the stuff Americans are made of, and when exercised makes a big man out of a boy, and has been demonstrated in millions of lives of the boys we sent over to finish what looked like a hopeless job for the rest of our Allies, or Associates.[31]

Additional notes in the *Independent Register* reported that in mid-May 1919, Skinner was showing a collection of photographs that a French comrade had taken on the battlefields of France. By early June he had returned to his previous employment with a Chicago life insurance company.[32]

Epilogue

It is only natural to wonder what happened to these men who sacrificed much to serve their country. While a complete accounting of each of them is beyond the scope of this story, a few details are in order.

Roger Skinner married in 1924 and, as of the census of 1930, had one adopted daughter. He was living in the Milwaukee area at that time and sold insurance. Skinner died young; he was forty-six years old when he died in 1936.[1]

Wilbert Murphy, from Brodhead, died there at the age of eighty-four. He had married but had no children and spent his life as a teacher. In 1930 Murphy was teaching in Freeport, Illinois; in 1940 he was a "commercial teacher" in West Allis, near Milwaukee.[2]

Reuel Barlow had both a family and fine career as a journalist and later as a professor of journalism at the University of Illinois. Barlow retired to California and died there at the age of seventy-four.[3]

Otis O'Brien lived to the age of seventy-one. As a young man he worked for the Advance Rumley Co., which produced tractors. He spent two years working for Rumley in Puerto Rico before moving with the company to Pennsylvania in 1923. O'Brien later taught at the University of Arizona and retired in Tucson.[4]

Those who fought and died in the war are remembered by members of the local historical societies and with books and monuments. The legion hall in Monticello is named after Fred Amstutz, who was killed in France; the legion hall in Brooklyn is named after Ben Johnson, who died of pneumonia in training. The Civics Club of Brodhead published a book in 1921 to honor all of the "Men of the Service" from Brodhead.[5]

The small towns that were once so full of life have changed substantially, although their main streets don't look so very different than they did one hundred years ago. Most of the businesses that people frequent are now in newer buildings on the edges of town. Brodhead still calls itself a "small city" and boasts a population of 3,200.[6] The old train depot in the center of town now houses the Brodhead Historical Society and its museum. Monticello and Brooklyn are smaller towns with populations of about 1,200 and 1,400, respectively. The Monticello Area Historical Society has moved into the drugstore on Main Street long owned by the Woefler family. Brooklyn also has an active historical society without a fixed address as of this writing.[7]

Small-town communities in Green County have struggled to hold on to their newspapers. The *Independent Register* maintains an office in "downtown" Brodhead, and its website masthead proclaims the continuous operation of the newspaper since 1860.[8] The once family-owned operation has recently been bought out and the space is now shared with a copy shop. The *Monticello Messenger* has merged with two other local newspapers. The *Post Messenger Recorder* is still delivered weekly by mail to loyal customers in town and on surrounding farms. The *Brooklyn Teller* was absorbed by the *Evansville Review* in the mid-1950s. Free newspapers with the primary purpose of advertising compete with these historic weeklies.

The content of the newspapers now differs substantially from that of a hundred years ago, but it still reflects a close community. Once these local newspapers provided county, state, and national news, in addition to news of more local interest. Sports news from the local public schools is now the main attraction. Local businesses, some of which trace their roots back nearly one hundred years, target advertising at suburbanites and farmers alike. Dairy farms still dominate the countryside in Green County, although they are fewer and larger than they were at the time of World War I. Residential neighborhoods now dot the gently rolling hills around Monticello and Brooklyn, not far from Madison.

All of the young men who took part in World War I are now gone. Though the Green County countryside has changed considerably since 1918, it would still be largely recognizable to the young men who went away to fight in Europe that year, could they see it now. Similarly, the stories they told and the experiences they related are at once unique and familiar to us. War is not usually fought on horseback anymore, nor is the army an all-male organization. The "aeroplanes" have changed in sophistication and the varieties of their appearance. Most of us will never have to know the terrors of going "over the top" to assault an enemy trench or run across no-man's-land with bullets and artillery shells slicing through the air and occasionally hitting home. Yet, in the accounts of these men as they looked for food after days of not eating, or passed the time with a French family with whom they could barely communicate, or as they struggled to reassure loved ones back home of their well-being and safety, we can see the bonds that still unite people, the everyday struggles we all face to provide for our families, and our efforts to learn of people different from us and get along as friends among those with whom we share little in common. In the words these young men shared through local newspapers—which are also becoming a thing of the past—World War I becomes something other than the nameless, faceless conglomerations of men and material that we often hear about, but instead a transformative experience as boys grew into men under the most trying of circumstances.

Notes

Introduction

1. David Zonderman, "Over Here: The Wisconsin Homefront during World War I," *Wisconsin Magazine of History* 77, no. 4 (Summer, 1994): 295–300; Lorin Lee Cary, "The Wisconsin Loyalty Legion, 1917–1918," *Wisconsin Magazine of History* 53, no. 1 (Autumn, 1969): 33–50; Karen Falk, "Public Opinion in Wisconsin During World War I," *Wisconsin Magazine of History* 25, no. 4 (June 1942): 389–407.
2. Fred L. Holmes, *Wisconsin's War Record* (Madison: Capital Historical Publishing Co., 1919). For draft response see Falk, "Public Opinion," 390. For percent of doctors in service, see Holmes, *Wisconsin's War Record*, 153. The corresponding number at the national level was 24 percent.
3. George Soule, *Prosperity Decade: From War to Depression, 1917–1929* (New York: Rinehart & Company, Inc., 1947); James L. Stokesbury, *A Short History of World War I* (1981; Repr., New York: Harper Collins Perennial, 2002): 310.
4. Robert H. Zieger, *America's Great War: World War I and the American Experience* (New York: Rowman and Littlefield, 2000), 108.
5. See John G. Gregory, *Wisconsin's Gold Star List: Soldiers, Sailors, Marines, and Nurses from the Badger State Who Died in the Federal Service During the World War* (Madison: State Historical Society of Wisconsin, 1925). Population data for the United States and Wisconsin, as of July 1918 from the US Census Bureau, was found on Google, Public Data: www .google.com/publicdata/explore?ds=kf7tgg1uo9ude_&hl=en&dl=en.
6. Earle William Gage, "Tractors That Fight on the West Front," *Tractor and Gas Engine Review* 11, no. 3 (March 1918): 9.
7. Chris Bishop, *The Illustrated Encyclopedia of Weapons of World War I: The Comprehensive Guide to Weapons Systems, Including Tanks, Small Arms, Warplanes, Artillery, Ships and Submarines* (London: Amber Books, 2014).
8. Zieger, *America's Great War*, 108–111.
9. See the front page of the *Independent Register*, August 22, September 12, and September 19, 1917, as well as that of the *Monticello Messenger*, September 12, 1917.
10. US Census Bureau, "Urban and Rural Population: 1900 to 1990," October 1995, www.census.gov/population/www/censusdata/files /urpop0090.txt.

11. Eric E. Lampard, *The Rise of the Dairy Industry in Wisconsin: A Study in Agricultural Change, 1820–1920* (Madison: The State Historical Society of Wisconsin, 1963), 96, 113, 295; *Memoirs of Green County, Wisconsin: From the Earliest Historical Times Down to the Present,* vol. 1 (Madison, WI: Central States Historical Association, 1913), 163.

12. Lampard, *Rise of the Dairy Industry,* 341.

13. Ibid., 160–162; *Memoirs of Green County,* 163.

14. US Department of Commerce, *14th Census of the United States, 1920,* vol. 6, *Agriculture: Reports for the States, with Statistics for Counties* (Washington, DC: Government Printing Office, 1920).

15. John D. Buenker, *The History of Wisconsin,* vol. 4, *The Progressive Era, 1893–1914* (Madison: State Historical Society of Wisconsin, 1998), 32–33.

16. US Department of Commerce, *14th Census of the United States, 1920,* vol. 3, *Population* (Washington, DC: Government Printing Office, 1920).

17. See *Memoirs of Green County,* 205–208, 239–242, 294–296, for histories of these three towns. The village of Brooklyn rests in two counties. A recorded 290 people from the village were in Green County in 1920 and the remainder (117) were in Dane County. "Brooklyn Has 407 Noses," *Brooklyn Teller,* September 8, 1920, 1.

18. With the exception of the cheese factories and the mills, these businesses all advertised together in a holiday greeting in the *Monticello Messenger,* January 3, 1917, 4. *N. W. Ayer & Son's American Newspaper Annual and Directory: A Catalogue of American Newspapers* (Philadelphia: N.W. Ayer & Son, 1916). Page 1047 notes the mills and cheese factories.

19. *Ayer & Son's American Newspaper Annual and Directory,* 103; *Memoirs of Green County,* 208. Large steam engines provided the power for electricity in Monticello; see "Electric Light Plant Now Running," *Monticello Messenger,* October 11, 1904, 1.

20. *Ayer & Son's American Newspaper Annual and Directory,* 1031.

21. *Memoirs of Green County,* 241.

22. Wisconsin as a whole was racially homogeneous: 99.4 percent white in 1920. US Census Bureau. US Department of Commerce, *14th Census of the United States, 1920,* vol. 3, *Population* (Washington, DC: Government Printing Office, 1920).

23. Falk, "Public Opinion," 394–395.

24. "Patriotic Mass Meeting," *Independent Register,* April 18, 1917, 1.

Chapter 1

1. "Plans to Raise United States Army of Two Million Men," *Brooklyn Teller,* May 16, 1917, 2; Zieger, *America's Great War,* 86; "Roll of Honor," *Brooklyn Teller,* May 2, 1917, 1.

2. "Wisconsin Guard to Mobilize," *Brooklyn Teller*, July 11, 1917, 1.
3. "R. Barlow Weds at Freeport," *Monticello Messenger*, July 18, 1917, 1.
4. Holmes, *Wisconsin's War Record*, 23.
5. Ibid.
6. "Bid Farewell to Wisconsin Guards," *Brooklyn Teller*, September 26, 1917, 1.
7. "Letter from Wilbert Murphy," *Brodhead News*, October 4, 1917, 1.
8. "Our Boys at the Front," *Independent Register*, November 28, 1917, 1
9. "From the Boys in the Colors," *Independent Register*, November 28, 1917, 1.
10. "Letter from Reuel R. Barlow," *Monticello Messenger*, November 7, 1917, 4.
11. "Our Boys at the Front," *Independent Register*, November 28, 1917, 1.
12. "Letter from Charles Marshall," *Independent Register*, January 16, 1918, 1.
13. "Ben Johnson Is Victim of Pneumonia," *Brooklyn Teller*, December 5, 1917, 1.
14. "Russell Agnew Writes," *Brodhead News*, February 14, 1918, 1.
15. "From Elmer Swann," *Brodhead News*, February 14, 1918, 1.
16. "Our Enlisted Boys," *Independent Register*, November 28, 1917, 1; Glenn Brazelton, *Company B, 119th Machine Gun Battalion, Price County's WWI Heroes*, Price County Historical Society, November 11, 2011, www.pricecountygenealogicalsociety.org/Books/119TH%20MG%20BN%20-%20FinalBookGBz.pdf.

Chapter 2
1. William G. Haan, "The Division as a Fighting Machine," *The Wisconsin Magazine of History* 4, no. 1 (September 1920): 3–26.
2. *The 32nd Division in the World War, 1917–1919*, issued by the Joint War History Commissions of Michigan and Wisconsin (Madison: Wisconsin War History Commission, 1920), 33.
3. "Brooklyn Soldiers Safely Across," *Brooklyn Teller*, March 13, 1918, 1.
4. "With the Colors," *Brooklyn Teller*, April 10, 1918, 1.
5. "Letter from Fred Amstutz," *Monticello Messenger*, April 17, 1918, 11.
6. "Letter from Clarence A. Bontly," *Monticello Messenger*, May 22, 1918, 4.
7. "Letters from 'Over There,'" *Monticello Messenger*, December 25, 1918, 8.
8. "From Wilbert Murphy," *Brodhead News*, March 6, 1919, 1.
9. "Letters from France," *Brooklyn Teller*, April 24, 1918, 1.
10. "Some Experiences of Russell Agnew," *Independent Register*, February 19, 1919, 1.
11. "From Charles R. Marshall," *Independent Register*, April 10, 1918, 1.
12. "From Wilbert Murphy," *Brodhead News*, April 4, 1918, 4.
13. "Reuel Barlow Writes Home," *Monticello Messenger*, April 10, 1918, 1.

14. "Letter from Reuel Barlow," *Monticello Messenger*, May 1, 1918, 5.
15. "From the Boys 'Over There,'" *Monticello Messenger*, June 5, 1918, 4.
16. "From Elmer Swann," *Independent Register*, May 29, 1918, 1; "From
    Elmer Swann," *Brodhead News*, June 6, 1918, 1; "From Elmer Swann,"
    Independent Register, June 12, 1918, 1; "From Elmer Swann," *Independent
    Register*, July 10, 1918, 1.
17. "Requartte Hahn Writes," *Brodhead News*, June 13, 1918, 4.
18. "From Requartte Hahn," *Independent Register*, June 12, 1918, 4.
19. Ibid.
20. Ibid.
21. "From the Boys 'Over There,'" *Monticello Messenger*, May 8, 1918, 5.
22. "From Wilbert Murphy," *Brodhead News*, June 6, 1918, 4.

Chapter 3
1. *The 32nd Division in the World War*, 34–35. By and large, the sergeants
   and commissioned officers of the 128th, as well as the unit name, stayed
   with the 32nd Division. Resources from across the division were real-
   located to return the 128th to some semblance of fighting strength. The
   32nd Division was comprised of four regiments, the 125th and 126th
   from Michigan and the 127th and 128th from Wisconsin.
2. "From Wilbert Murphy," *Independent Register*, June 5, 1918, 1.
3. "With the Colors," *Brooklyn Teller*, May 1, 1918, 1.
4. "Letters from France," *Brooklyn Teller*, April 24, 1918, 1.
5. "From Otis O'Brien," *Brooklyn Teller*, June 12, 1918, 1.
6. The 32nd Division was assigned to the tenth training area with headquarters in Prauthoy, about 320 kilometers southeast of Paris. New
   River Notes, "Order of Battle, American Forces, World War I," www
   .newrivernotes.com/topical_history_ww1_oob_american_forces.htm.
   It's not clear where the hospital was or why Bernie was hospitalized. It
   might have been influenza or an injury from construction work.
7. "With the Colors," *Brooklyn Teller*, June 28, 1918, 1.
8. Ibid., September 12, 1918, 1.
9. Ibid., August 7, 1918, 1.
10. *The 32nd Division in the World War*, 41–50.
11. "Writes from the Trenches," *Monticello Messenger*, August 7, 1918, 1.
12. "Fred Amstutz Gives His All," *Monticello Messenger*, August 28, 1918, 1.
13. "From Elmer Swann," *Independent Register*, September 4, 1918, 1.
14. "Letters from Reuel Barlow," *Monticello Messenger*, September 11, 1918, 1.
15. "With the Colors," *Brooklyn Teller*, September 19, 1918, 1.
16. Ibid. .
17. Ibid.

18. Major General William G. Haan, "The Division as a Fighting Machine," *The Wisconsin Magazine of History* 4, no. 1 (September 1920): 10.
19. "With the Colors," *Brooklyn Teller*, September 19, 1918, 1.
20. Ibid., October 17, 1918, 1.
21. Ibid., October 24, 1918, 1.
22. "From Requartte Hahn," *Independent Register*, September 25, 1918, 1.
23. "The Liberty Bond Report," *Monticello Messenger*, October 31, 1917, 1; "Red Cross List Growing," *Monticello Messenger*, October 31, 1917, 1.
24. "Monroe Paper Takes Hard Slam at Monticello," *Monticello Messenger*, October 24, 1917, 1.
25. "2d Liberty Loan Is Being Pushed," *Brooklyn Teller*, October 10, 1917, 1.
26. "From Charles Marshall," *Independent Register*, June 12, 1918, 1.
27. "Requartte Hahn Writes," *Brodhead News*, June 13, 1918, 4. I verified Requartte Hahn's ancestry in Ancestry at www.ancestry.com. When I search under the terms "Requartte Hahn," and "Wisconsin" the results turned up entries from the 1910 and 1920 population censuses. Both entries confirm that Hahn's parents were born in Wisconsin but both grandfathers were born in Germany.
28. "Tells of Boche Barbarity," *Monticello Messenger*, August 28, 1918, 1.
29. "From the Boys 'Over There,'" *Monticello Messenger*, September 18, 1918, 1.
30. "Many Attend Meetings," *Monticello Messenger*, March 20, 1918, 1; "German Show Coming," *Monticello Messenger*, April 3, 1918, 8.
31. "Makes Call on Pro-Germans," *Monticello Messenger*, July 10, 1918, 1.
32. The Sam Browne belt is a wide leather belt with a narrow supporting strap passing over the right shoulder.
33. "32nd Fights to 'On Wisconsin,'" *Brodhead News*, October 17, 1918, 1; "32nd Fights to 'On Wisconsin' (continued from last week)," *Brodhead News*, October 24, 1918, 1.
34. "32nd Fights to 'On Wisconsin' (continued from last week)," *Brodhead News*, October 24, 1918, 1.
35. *The 32nd Division in the World War*, 88–89; "The 32nd 'Red Arrow' Division in World War I: From the 'Iron Jaw' Division to 'Les Terribles,'" The 32nd Division Veterans Association, www.32nd-division.org/history/ww1/32-ww1.html.
36. "Americans Fire French Guns Six Times Faster Than the French, Says Reuel Barlow," *Monticello Messenger*, November 6, 1918, 1
37. Ibid.
38. "From Requartte Hahn," *Independent Register*, November 13, 1918, 1.
39. Both letters are found in the same story, "Letter from Reuel Barlow," *Monticello Messenger*, November 27, 1918, 1.

40. The 301st Tank Battalion went into action in late September. See several letters in the *Independent Register*: "From Elmer Dixon," April 24, 1918, 1; "From Sergt Elmer Dixon," May 22, 1918, 1; "From Sergt Elmer Dixon," June 12, 1918, 1; and "From Sergt Elmer Dixon," July 3, 1918, 1. The Great War Society, Doughboy Center, www.worldwar1.com/dbc /tanks.htm.

41. "From Elmer Dixon," *Brodhead News*, December 5, 1918, 1.

42. New River Notes, "Order of Battle, American Forces, World War I," www.newrivernotes.com/topical_history_ww1_oob_american _forces.htm.

43. "Captain Praises Sam Schmid," *Monticello Messenger*, July 3, 1918, 1.

44. "From Wilbert Murphy," *Independent Register*, July 17, 1918, 1.

45. Ibid., September 11, 1918, 1.

46. Ibid., November 6, 1918, 1.

47. "With the Colors," *Brooklyn Teller*, August 21, 1918, 1.

48. Ibid., October 24, 1918, 1.

49. Ibid., November 17, 1918, 1.

Chapter 4

1. "The 32nd Red Arrow Division in World War 1," The 32nd Red Arrow Veteran Association, www.32nd-division.org/history/ww1/32-ww1 .html.

2. "1st Infantry Division (United States)," Wikipedia, http://en.wikipedia .org/wiki/1st_Infantry_Division_%28United_States%29.

3. Robert H. Zieger, *America's Great War* (New York: Rowman & Little-field, 2000), 108–111.

4. "From Wilbert Murphy," *Brodhead News*, November 7, 1918, 1.

5. "From Corp Burdette Purdy," *Independent Register*, September 11, 1918, 1.

6. Ibid., January 15, 1919, 1. Purdy eventually made it back to Wisconsin and worked in Racine "in the employ of the U.S. Express service." See "The Boys with the Colors," *Independent Register*, June 4, 1919, 1.

7. "From Serg Warren Niles," *Independent Register*, January 1, 1919, 1.

8. "With the Colors," *Brooklyn Teller*, October 24, 1918, 1.

9. Ibid., November 7, 1918, 1.

10. Ibid., December 26, 1918, 1.

11. Ibid., October 11, 1918, 1.

12. Ibid., February 12, 1919, 1.

13. Ibid.

14. "Corp Agnew Writes," *Brodhead News*, April 3, 1919, 1.

15. "From Russell Agnew," *Brodhead News*, November 28, 1918, 1.

16. Ibid., December 5, 1918, 1.

17. Ibid.
18. "From Elmer Swann," *Independent Register*, May 29, 1918, 1, and June 12, 1918, 1.
19. "From Elmer Swann," *Brodhead News*, September 12, 1918, 1.
20. "Boys with the Colors," *Independent Register*, September 25, 1918, 1.
21. "From Elmer Swann," *Independent Register*, January 1, 1919, 1.
22. Ibid., January 15, 1919, 1.
23. "More Soldiers Home," *Brodhead News*, February 20, 1919, 4; "Boys with the Colors," *Independent Register*, May 28, 1919, 1.
24. "From Miss Mae Howe," *Independent Register*, October 9, 1918, 1.
25. Ibid., September 11, 1918, 1, and October 9, 1918, 1.
26. "Leonard W. Rhyner," *Monticello Messenger*, November 20, 1918, 1.
27. Steven Burg, "Wisconsin and the Great Spanish Flu Epidemic of 1918," *Wisconsin Magazine of History* 84, no. 1 (Autumn 2000): 37–56; John M. Barry, *The Great Influenza: The Epic Story of the Deadliest Plague in History* (New York: Penguin Books, 2004), 231–240; Zieger, *America's Great War*, 108.
28. Burg, "Wisconsin and the Great Spanish Flu Epidemic," 41–42; Barry, *The Great Influenza*, 182, 306; "The Boys with the Colors," *Independent Register*, October 9, 1918, 1.
29. "Obituary—Clara H. Peterson," *Brooklyn Teller*, October 31, 1918, 1; "Called Home," *Brooklyn Teller*, December 12, 1918, 1; "Carol Livingston," *Brodhead News*, December 12, 1918, 1.
30. "With the Colors," *Brooklyn Teller*, November 21, 1918, 1, and January 29, 1919, 1.
31. "With the Colors," *Brooklyn Teller*, January 16, 1919, 1; "Letters from the Boys 'Over There,'" *Monticello Messenger*, January 29, 1919, 1.
32. Burg, "Wisconsin and the Great Spanish Flu Epidemic"; "Flu Ban on Again," *Brodhead News*, December 19, 1918, 1.

Chapter 5
1. "Monticello Wild with Joy over Peace News," *Monticello Messenger*, November 13, 1918, 1.
2. "With the Colors," *Brooklyn Teller*, December 12, 1918, 1.
3. Ibid., December 19, 1918, 9.
4. Ibid., December 5, 1918, 1.
5. Ibid., January 9, 1919, 1.
6. "From Elmer Dixon," *Independent Register*, December 25, 1918, 1.
7. *The 32nd Division in the World War*, 127–140.
8. "Letters from 'Over There,'" *Monticello Messenger*, January 1, 1919, 1.
9. Ibid., February 5, 1919, 1.

Chapter 6

1. "From Chas Marshall," *Independent Register*, February 19, 1919, 1, 8.
2. "From Rex Hahn," *Brodhead News*, February 13, 1919, 1.
3. "From Wilbert Murphy," *Brodhead News*, March 6, 1919, 1.
4. "Five Days I Will Never Forget," *Independent Register*, March 26, 1919, 1.
5. "Boys Long to Return Home," *Monticello Messenger*, March 5, 1919, 1.
6. "With the Colors," *Brooklyn Teller*, May 21, 1919, 1.
7. Ibid. Others who arrived home in May included Russell Agnew, Requartte Hahn, Charles Marshall, Elmer Swann, and Edwin Barlow. "Welcome Home for 32nd Div," *Independent Register*, May 21, 1919, 1; "The Boys with the Colors," *Independent Register*, May 28, 1919, 1. Ernest Wirth of Monticello arrived home before May 14, according to the *Monticello Messenger*, May 14, 1919, 1.
8. Brooklyn boys who marched in their hometown Memorial Day parade included Bernie Christensen, Arnold Hansen, Einar Johnson, Otis O'Brien, Ray Olson, and Albert Weisser. "Soldiers in Brooklyn Memorial Day," *Brooklyn Teller*, June 11, 1919, 1.
9. "From Elmer Dixon," *Independent Register*, April 2, 1919, 1; "Soldiers Return Home," *Brodhead News*, April 17, 1919, 1. Dixon was expected to resume a business in Albany "in the near future." "The Boys with the Colors," *Independent Register*, April 23, 1919, 1.
10. "The Boys with the Colors," *Independent Register*, July 16, 1919, 1; Brodhead News, July 3, 1919, 5; "More Soldiers Home," *Brodhead News*, July 17, 1919, 4.
11. "Brothers Meet in Germany," *Monticello Messenger*, March 19, 1919, 1; "Reuel Barlow Now in Paris," *Monticello Messenger*, April 3, 1919, 1; "The Boys with the Colors," *Independent Register*, August 13, 1919, 1, and September 10, 1919, 1.

Part II

1. Several articles from the *Independent Register* provided background information on Skinner's life including: "From Roger Skinner Now in Europe," *Independent Register*, September 19, 1917, 1, "From Roger Skinner," January 23, 1918, 1, and "The Boys with the Colors," June 4, 1919, 1. I found his birth year on "Find a Grave," at www.findagrave.com /cgi-bin/fg.cgi/page/gr/fg.cgi?page=gr&GRid=157917949. The name of his father matched that given in the news articles, so I was sure I had the right Roger A. Skinner. For more information on Skinner, see Note 1 for Epilogue.
2. "From Roger Skinner Now in Europe," *Independent Register*, September 19, 1917, 1.

3. "From Roger Skinner," *Brodhead News*, September 20, 1917, 4.
4. "From Roger Skinner," *Independent Register*, November 21, 1917, 1.
5. Ibid., November 7, 1917, 1.
6. Ibid., December 26, 1917, 1.
7. Ibid., January 23, 1918, 1.
8. Ibid., March 6, 1918, 1.
9. Ibid., March 27, 1918, 1.
10. Ibid., April 17, 1918, 1.
11. Ibid., 1, 8.
12. Ibid., 8.
13. "From Roger Skinner," *Independent Register*, May 18, 1918, 1.
14. Ibid., May 22, 1918, 1.
15. Ibid.
16. "From Roger Skinner," *Independent Register*, June 12, 1918, 1.
17. Ibid., July 24, 1918, 1.
18. Ibid., July 3, 1918, 1.
19. Ibid., July 24, 1918, 1.
20. Ibid., August 28, 1918, 1.
21. Ibid.
22. "From Roger Skinner," *Independent Register*, October 16, 1918, 1.
23. Ibid., November 27, 1918, 1.
24. Ibid., December 4, 1918, 1.
25. Ibid., December 25, 1918, 1.
26. Ibid., January 8, 1919, 1.
27. Ibid.
28. "The Boys with the Colors," *Independent Register*, January 8, 1919, 1.
29. "From Roger Skinner," *Independent Register*, March 5, 1919, 1.
30. "The Boys with the Colors," *Independent Register*, April 9, 1919, 1.
31. "Sergeant Roger Skinner Home," *Independent Register*, May 21, 1919, 1.
32. "The Boys with the Colors," *Independent Register*, May 21, 1919, 1, and June 4, 1919, 1.

Epilogue

1. Armed with birth and death years found online at "Find a Grave," see Note 1 for Part II above, I searched on Ancestry for more information on Roger Skinner's life. Using the terms "Roger A Skinner," "Wisconsin," and birth date of "1890," I searched at www.ancestry.com. The search turned up several items including the 1930 census record (with an image of the original hand-written entry) that revealed family members and occupation.

2. I found information on Wilbert Murphy by searching "wilbert murphy green county Wisconsin" on Google. I was referred to death records for Wilbert Murphy on "Mooseroots, by Graphiq" death notice page at http://death-records.mooseroots.com/d/n/Wilbert-Murphy. I learned that Wilbert Murphy from Brodhead, Wisconsin, was born on July 31, 1898, and died on February 1, 1982. I then searched on www.ancestry .com, using the terms "Wilbert Murphy," "Brodhead, Wisconsin" and birth date of "1898." The Ancestry search turned up census records from the 1930 and 1940 censuses where I found the information contained here.
3. Reuel Barlow can also be found at www.ancestry.com by searching "Reuel Barlow" "Wisconsin." A search on Newspapers.com turned up the following published articles: "Veteran Returns to Scene of Armistice 17 Years After" *The Decatur (Illinois) Daily Review*, November 10, 1935, 11; and "Former U of I Prof Dies in California" *The Southern Illinoisan* (Carbondale, Illinois), May 5, 1968, 4.
4. I found information on Otis O'Brien searching on www.ancestry.com using the terms "Otis O'Brien" "Wisconsin." Among the items that turned up was the census record from 1910 where Otis and his brother Lyle (frequently mentioned in letters) were both included in the household. I learned that Otis was born approximately in 1896 since he was listed as 14 years old. A search on Newspapers.com delivered an obituary from the Janesville Daily Gazette: "Southern Wisconsin Obituaries," *Janesville (Wisconsin) Daily Gazette*, October 5, 1965, 2. The personals column of the same paper in 1923 had an interesting note about his employment in Puerto Rico. "Personals," March 24, 1923, 2. Search items in my original Ancestry search verified that he traveled back and forth to Puerto Rico.
5. The Civics Club, *Brodhead's Tribute to Her Men of the Service, 1914–1918* (Madison: Cantwell Printing Co., 1921). The book included one woman among those honored: Marjorie Faye Skinner. She had been a teacher and she served in Washington, DC, with the navy attached to the USS *Triton*.
6. City of Brodhead, "About," www.cityofbrodheadwi.us/general /index.php.
7. Brodhead Historical Society, www.brodheadhistory.org/; Monticello Area Historical Society, www.monticellohistoricalsociety.org/; Brooklyn Area Historical Society Facebook page, www.facebook.com/bahswi.
8. *The Independent Register/The Clinton Topper*, http://indreg.com/.

Index

Salvation Army, 90
Sam Browne belts, 68
Schmid, Sam, 82
searchlights, 3, 56, 68, 132, 164
seasickness, 27–28, 134
Second Battle of the Marne. *See*
Aisne-Marne Campaign
"Sedition Map," **59**
service stripes, 131, 167
shell holes, 66, 70, 88, 173
shells and bombs: and ambulance
runs, 170–171, 172–173, 175–176;
in ambulance unit camp area,
180; artillery shells, 3; "duds,"
54, 56; French, 156; German
bombing raids, 43, 58, 62, 63–64;
Murphy on shell fire, 82, 83; near
Juvigny, France, 94–95; nerves
affected, 83, 94, 120; on roads,
189–190; Soissons front, 124–
125, 127, 128; star shells, 43; submarine attacks, 13, 141, 143–145;
"well diggers," 56, 77
shoes and boots, 21–22, 153, 168, 200
shrapnel, 62, 79, 82, 125, 180, 181
sight seeing: France, 183, 184; Germany, 131–132; New York City,
24
singing, 63, 140, 152, 185
Skinner, Mr. and Mrs. W. R., 138, 199
Skinner, Roger A., 6; after the war,
202; aid for soldiers in France,
90; and armistice, 192–199
background, 137–138; at base
hospital near Paris, 145–147;
Christmas 1917, 150–153; eligible for French Cross, 196; first
impressions of France, 142–143;
on French hospitality, 160–161;
on gas attack ambulance run,
153–155; passage to France,
139–145; rest days, 183–185;
return home, 199–201; train
transport, 178–179; travel days,
166–169, 188; work as an ambulance driver, 147–150, 156–159,
161–165, 170–177, 179–192

sleep: ambulance drivers, **152**, 168;
in dugouts, 48; and gas attacks,
41, 56; and night attacks, 120; at
Soissons front, 126
Smith, Boyd, 88
snow. *See* winter weather
Soissons front, 76, 78, 82, 93, 96,
119–120, 121–122, 121–128
soldiers, nature of, 119–120
Sopwith Camel (British biplane
fighter), **125**
souvenirs, 191, 200–201
Spanish flu, 89, 100–102, 115, 176,
201
St. Mihiel, battle of, 82, **84**, 87, 94,
189, **189**
St. Quentin, France, 107, 108
St. Uasse, France, 108
star shells, 43
Stars and Stripes (newspaper), 78
stretchers and stretcher-bearers,
66–68, 158
submarines, 13, 141, 143–145
supply companies, 53–56, 84,
106–107
supply depot, German bombing attempt, 43
surgical hospitals, 65–68, 96, 118–119
surgical operations (medical proce-
dures), 66, 67, 118–119
Swann, Elmer: in Alsace, 47–48;
on being wounded, 96–97; first
impressions of France, 34–36,
95; hospital work, 34, 61; on T.
Roosevelt, 25; on visit to New
York City, 24
Swann, Lee, 95

tanks and tank repair, 75, 80–81, **80**,
107–108, 124
tear gas, 23
technology, war applications of, 2–3
tents, 174
Thompson, Harold, 101, 134
Thompson, Lieutenant, 62
tobacco, mailed from home, 38,
153–154

About the Author

Carrie A. Meyer is an associate professor of economics at George Mason University and has been a full-time faculty member since 1988. Before completing a PhD in economics at the University of Illinois, Meyer was a Peace Corps volunteer in the Dominican Republic. Much of her research has focused on the agriculture, environment,  and institutions of the developing world, about which she has written numerous papers, books, and reports. Since November, 2000, Meyer has focused her research on the history of the rural Midwest, which resulted in her book *Days on the Family Farm*, published by University of Minnesota Press in 2007. Her article "Wisconsin's Gas Engines" appeared in the *Wisconsin Magazine of History* in spring 2016.